Y0-AAG-477

Who do we *try to* <u>RESCUE</u> today?

by Ed Finn

published by
Canadian Centre for Policy Alternatives

Copyright © 2000 Ed Finn and Canadian Centre for Policy Alternatives

All rights reserved. No part of this book may be reproduced or transmitted in any form or by any means, electronic or mechanical, including photocopying, or by any information storage or retrieval system, without permission in writing from the author or publisher.

Canadian Cataloguing in Publication Data

Finn, Ed, 1926-
Who do we try to rescue today?: Canada under corporate rule

ISBN 0-88627-217-3

1. Business and politics–Canada 2. Canada–Politics and government–1993- 3. Canada–Economic policy–1991-
4. Canada–Social policy. I. Canadian Centre for Policy Alternatives. II. Title.

HD2809.F55 2000   322'.3'0971   C00-900286-3

Printed and Bound in Canada

Published by
Canadian Centre for Policy Alternatives
410-75 Albert Street
Ottawa, Ontario K1P 5E7
tel: 613-563-1341
email: ccpa@policyalternatives.ca
http://www.policyalternatives.ca

TABLE OF CONTENTS

FOREWORD

The title of this book is taken from one of my columns in *Canadian Forum* a few years ago [*you'll find it on Page 87*]. Many readers of that magazine seemed to be struck by the concept of a river full of the drowning victims of "the free market," and the frantic efforts of social action groups to rescue them.

I thought this metaphor was appropriate to apply to all the pieces in this anthology. The river of Canadian society is still sweeping away the growing legions of the poor, the homeless, the hungry, and the other outcasts of a ruthless global economy. And most of the groups set up to help them still seem more preoccupied with pulling them out of the river than trying to prevent them from being thrown in.

This is the second collection of essays on the subject of globalization that I have had the immodesty to compile. The first one, *Under Corporate Rule,* sold about 2,000 copies since it came out in 1996, and you might feel its 35,000 words were enough to exhaust my thinking on this subject. You could be right, since I have reworked a few items from that first volume and integrated them into this one to fill in a few gaps; but 90 per cent of the material in this book was produced over the past four years and reflects my ongoing concern (some might call it obsession) with the baneful effects of the New World Order.

As a writer, I wasn't always so fixated. Indeed, up to the 1990s, my columns were quite eclectic. But, as the big corporations grew in size and power, and as their power began to stifle true democracy, it became more and more difficult to write about any economic, social or political issue without relating it to the overriding reality of corporate rule.

I suppose there are still some topics that lend themselves to being written about fairly and fully outside of this grim reality. Sports and cultural events come to mind, although even in these spheres the influence of corporate and financial forces are becoming decisive. Certainly, any commentator these days who ignores or underrates the dominant role of corporate power in our society does not deserve to be taken seriously.

The essays that follow reflect various aspects of Canadian life under corporate rule in the dying years of the 20th century. Their overall intent is first to inform, second to infuriate, third to encourage, and fourth to galvanize.

Only an informed, dedicated, militant, and mobilized populace can challenge and eventually topple our corporate rulers. If this book helps in some small way to inspire such a popular uprising, it will have justified its publication.

My thanks to all my colleagues at the CCPA for their help with this project (especially my daughter Kerri-Anne, who did the layout), and to my friends Tony Clarke, Murray Dobbin, Mel Hurtig, Maude Barlow, Heather-jane Robertson and Colleen Fuller, whose most recent books have exposed the deleterious effects of corporate rule on key sectors of our society. They all share my concerns about globalization, but again I should make it clear that they do not necessarily agree with all of my arguments or conclusions. Responsibility for the views expressed in these pages is therefore mine alone.

The price of silence

When they came for the poor and homeless,
    I was silent, because I was well-off.
When they came for the pensioners,
    I was silent because I had a good RRSP.
When they came for the unemployed,
    I was silent because I had a job.
When they came for the homeless,
    I was silent because I had a home.
When they came for the immigrants,
    I was silent because I was born here.
When they came for the sick and disabled,
    I was silent because I was healthy.
When they came for the women,
    I was silent because I was male.
When they came for the children,
    I was silent because I was grown up.
When they came for the students,
    I was silent because I had my degree.
When they came for the youth,
    I was silent because I was middle-aged.
When they came for the Aboriginal peoples,
    I was silent because I was Anglo-Saxon.

When at last they came for me,
    No one was left to hear my cries.

    —With thanks and apologies to the late
    Bishop Martin Niemoller.

PART I

Corporate Rule: Accomplished

The corporate coup d'état
A crazy conspiracy theory?
The corporate cancer
Free trade fiasco
Free trade: still the No. 1 concern
Bread and circuses
"Money is like manure"
How the IMF started the war in Kosovo

The corporate coup d'état

A coup d'état, especially a non-violent one, can't succeed without a shrewd, careful, long-term strategy. The takeover of Canada by its big business executives could not have been achieved if they had not planned it so brilliantly. Even a shade less forethought, less daring, less patience, less attention to detail could have aborted their mission before it was accomplished.

Before discussing the various stages and elements of their grand design, let's concede that Canada's top CEOs had a lot of help from the new computer technologies and the globalization of business and finance they helped unleash. To some extent, these developments alone would have boosted corporate power considerably. But to seize absolute power, an elaborate takeover plan was still required.

Conceived in the mid-1970s by corporate leaders chafing under political, regulatory, jurisdictional and labour constraints, it aimed to bring Canada under corporate rule within the next two decades. This had to be done quietly, stealthily, incrementally, to avert the mobilization of effective opposition. It had to be given the appearance of a natural evolution, driven by impersonal and inexorable global forces.

The first and most important step, then, was to influence public opinion. The CEOs knew from their product marketing campaigns that people's preferences could be shaped by slick advertising. They knew that people's thinking about economic and social issues could be similarly manipulated by the same techniques. Repeated and heard often enough, the biggest lies become unquestioned beliefs.

Here, then, in rough chronological order, are the steps and stages that comprised the corporate strategy.

1. Get organized. To coordinate the various elements of their plan, the CEOs of the 150 largest corporations set up and generously funded the Business Council on National Issues. The BCNI was to be the "quarterback" in planning and executing their long-term offensive.

2. Set up or co-opt conservative think-tanks. The corporate agenda had to be given academic credibility. This became the primary role of the Fraser and C.D. Howe Institutes, whose officers and minions quickly became adept at giving economic statistics the required right-wing spin.

3. Develop and cultivate articulate spokespeople. BCNI president Tom d'Aquino adroitly fills this role, supported by such high-profile media "neo-cons" as Jeffrey Simpson, David Frum, Terence Corcoran, Peter Cook, Diane Francis, Barbara Amiel and Andrew Coyne, academics such as John Crispo, Michael Bliss and William Watson, and of course the ubiquitous Michael Walker of the Fraser Institute.

4. Create and control the terminology. The terms coined by the neo-cons—e.g., "big government," "the nanny state," "the debt/deficit crisis," "welfare cheats," "special interest groups," "globalization," "competitiveness," "economic restructuring," "downsizing," etc.—have come to dominate public discourse, forcing those on the left to debate key issues in the language of the right.

5. Control the media. This was easy. Most newspapers, magazines, and radio and TV stations, after all, are owned by BCNI members. Three newspaper moguls—Conrad Black, Ken Thomson and Paul Desmarais—now own or control 72 of Canada's 110 dailies. The same concentration of corporate power prevails in the broadcast media (except for the CBC), and in magazines. Little wonder that news and views that support the corporate agenda flow easily through the media, while the voices of dissent get scant space or time, and are mostly confined to publications (such as *The CCPA Monitor* and the *Canadian Forum*) that reach relatively few people.

6. Control or coerce all political parties. This was not so difficult, either. The Liberal, Tory and Reform parties, being mainly run by and for the corporations anyway, proved willing—even eager—to help advance the corporate agenda. Business chiefs such as Brian Mulroney, Michael Wilson, Jean Chrétien and Paul Martin took sabbaticals from their executive suites to assume political leadership on behalf of the BCNI. The NDP, when it came to power in a province, was either duped and converted to neoconservatism by the right-wing propaganda blitz, or was frightened into compliance by the threat of a massive business exodus and/or an engineered financial crisis. Thus the CEOs could be confident that their agenda would continue to be implemented politically, no matter which party was favoured by the voters.

7. Achieve maximum corporate mobility. This was done mainly by having their political puppets negotiate first the Canada-U.S. Free Trade Agreement (FTA) and then the North American Free Trade Agreement (NAFTA). Promoted as free trade deals, their chief purpose was to enable the corporations to go anywhere in the world to exploit the cheapest labour and lowest taxes, to "shed" Canadian workers, and even to relocate their plants abroad and still send their goods back to Canada duty-free. Of course the development of high-tech communications technologies also gave them world-wide financial mobility.

8. Escape from legal restrictions. Regulations that forced the corporations to abide by certain minimal standards—product quality, health and safety, pollution, service to the public, consumer protection, and so on—were incompatible with the goal of total corporate freedom. They had to be eliminated, or at least reduced to token levels. So, one by one, nearly all the major industries have been deregulated. The corporations have been set free to "regulate" themselves, as if "good corporate citizenship" in the 1990s had not become the most ironic of oxymorons.

9. Dismantle the public sector. By creating and then demonizing "the debt/deficit crisis," the CEOs and their tame politicians and P.R. experts gave themselves the all-purpose excuse to slash government spending on social programs. Over the past 15 years they have rampaged through the public sector, privatizing services, getting rid of those they can't privatize, laying off public employees, and subjecting health care, education and social assistance to the death of a thousand cuts. Private sector rule means public sector subjugation.

10. Disarm and weaken the opposition. The right-wing propagandists have done a good job of discrediting and even ridiculing any person or organization daring to oppose the corporate agenda. They are dismissed as cranks or troublemakers, as special interest groups, as welfare state parasites, as Luddites foolishly trying to keep the economy from growing. To make sure they don't seriously threaten corporate rule, unemployment is kept very high and unemployment insurance and welfare payments very low. If the dissidents' NGOs are dependent on government funding, that funding is cut or completely withdrawn.

10. Curb the rights and effectiveness of organized labour. One of the few corporate objectives that have so far been stymied in Canada has been the enfeeblement of the labour movement. Granted, union strength has been sapped to some extent by the rising power of the corporations, by keeping a few million people jobless, and by having governments curb collective bargaining and freeze wages in the public sector. Still, union members refuse to abandon their unions, and in recent years have even shown signs of renewed militancy. It can be only a matter of time, however, before the

CEOs and their political sychophants resort to more brutal anti-labour tactics. The signs of that more aggressive treatment of unionized workers are already evident in Ontario, the province most rapidly being transformed into a police state.

11. Exalt and protect the value of wealth. The underlying goal of the corporate agenda, the one that subsumes all others, is to protect the wealthy and make them wealthier. The normal workings of unfettered free enterprise have that effect, in any case, but other safeguards include keeping interest rates high and inflation low, imposing little or no tax on wealth, allowing it to be invested freely outside the country, giving the wealthy elevated social status and privilege, and of course providing them with riot squad protection from their resentful victims.

12. Preserve the illusion of democracy. This is quite a feat, considering how absolute corporate rule has become in this country; but so far the CEOs have managed to pull it off. They do it mainly by preserving the outward trappings of a democratic state. We still have several political parties, still have "free" elections, still have legislatures in session. Protesters are still free to demonstrate, free to lobby their MPs and MLAs, free to present briefs to parliamentary committees. They can even, occasionally, get their alternative views reported in the media. For most Canadians—even the dissidents themselves—the exercise of these traditional democratic "freedoms" is enough to maintain the illusion of a true democracy. In reality, they are no more substantive than a politician's promise, no more real than a TV soap opera. They work because most of us accept the illusion as reality. ❖

A crazy conspiracy theory?

There's this cartoon about two cows. The first cow has just figured out how hamburgers are made.

The second cow scoffs at her: "You leftists and your crazy conspiracy theories!"

I keep thinking about this cartoon as I see the "new world order" taking shape around me. It is not really new, of course. It is starting to resemble the mid-Victorian sweatshop era— the heyday of the corporate robber barons.

That period was characterized by high levels of poverty and unemployment, by low wages, by weak or nonexistent unions, by wide economic and social disparities. Governments acted solely in the interests of powerful business and upper-class élites.

A century of progress to a more enlightened and egalitarian society couldn't be reversed easily or quickly. It is taking a couple of decades. But the present-day robber barons—the trans-national corporations (TNCs)—are well on the way toward reaching their retrogressive goal.

With the help of their compliant political puppets, they've already constrained collective bargaining and ratcheted down wages. Their free trade agreements have wiped out hundreds of thousands of middle-income jobs, creating a horde of unemployed desperate enough to work for poverty-level pay.

Cuts in unemployment insurance benefits make doubly sure the jobless don't get too picky about taking the menial or part-time work they're now being offered. But it's not just UI that must be slashed. If Canada is to become a low-wage country, as the TNCs have decreed, the entire social safety net will have to be shredded—social assistance, welfare, family support programs, health care, education, anything that might make people less vulnerable to "market forces."

Besides, a low-wage country can't generate the tax income needed to support social programs, so they'd have to go, anyway.

So will universal access to secondary education and skills-upgrading. Why educate or retrain people for high-tech, high-paying jobs that no longer exist—the kind of jobs the TNCs have no intention of providing in Canada any more? These are middle-class jobs, and we're well on the way to getting rid of our middle class. In a low-wage country, there are only two classes—the rich and the poor. Look at almost any Third World nation if you want to see where Canada is being slowly but surely herded.

At this point, most readers who have gotten this far will be dismissing me and my fantastic leftist conspiracy theory. I've gone well beyond their limits of credulity. They find it inconceivable that their country's decline could be the result of a coldly calculated plot. Why on Earth, they wonder, would the big business potentates deliberately convert Canada from a prosperous to an impoverished nation?

The TNCs' explanation for our economic woes is much more plausible, if you don't challenge it. We're the victims of uncontrollable market trends and forces, they tell us. Globalization is inevitable. So is "restructuring." So is low-wage and low-cost competitiveness. So are leaner employers and meaner governments. So is higher unemployment and poverty. "None of these unpleasant developments," they piously proclaim, "have anything to do with us."

Personally, I find this blameless big business theory a lot harder to swallow than mine. But it does have the advantage of being solemnly endorsed and defended by legions of reputable academics, politicians, think tanks, editorial writers, and of course all the boards of trade and chambers of commerce. Given that kind of sweeping acceptance, it's easy to lump the few dissenters like me in with the Flat Earth Society.

But wait a minute. Isn't it the corporations that are laying off people and moving their plants out of Canada? Isn't it the corporations that are demanding (and getting) wage concessions? That pushed hardest for free trade and the GST? That demanded the privatization and sale of Petro-Canada and Air Canada? That fought for the deregulation of our transportation and communications industries? That lobbied for (and got) multi-billion-dollar tax breaks? That keep telling us we can no longer afford our "too-generous" social services?

These activities are not passive. They don't conform with the theory that the corporations, like the rest of us, are being swept along helplessly on a flood of impersonal and uncontrollable changes. On the contrary, the evidence is clear that they are the architects of these changes. Certainly, unlike most of us, they are pleased with the results.

The ancient Romans, when they wanted to understand what was happening and why, would ask: "Cui bono?" Who benefits? It's still a pertinent question. Who stands to gain from high unemployment, low wages, low business taxes, weak unions, the dismantling of the welfare state? The answer is clear: the transnational corporations and the minority of executives, administrators, professionals and shareholders who split their profits.

Let's not forget: these privileged few never did like unions or free collective bargaining. They fiercely opposed minimum wage and occupational health and safety laws. They fought every step in the creation of the welfare state, every regulation and standard that diminished their autocratic control of the work force.

They were dragged kicking and screaming into the 20th century, and they were never happy with it. That's why, suddenly given the opportunity and the power to do so, they are bent on making sure that the 21st century will be more like the 19th.

The power of the 19th-century corporations, you'll recall, was curbed by a combination of strong unions and reform-minded national governments. Together they managed to stop or moderate the worst excesses of unfettered capitalism. The rapid globalization of business, finances and trade, however, has freed the corporations from the constraints of labour and government, both of which are still largely confined within national boundaries.

The footloose TNCs can thus use their global mobility to set the conditions under which they will operate in any juris-diction: and those conditions, if met, will lead us inexorably backward—back to a neo-Victorian era where corporate power once more reigns supreme.

It's a counterrevolution that's well under way and gain-ing momentum; but it's not yet unstoppable. Granted, all current Canadian governments, willingly or not, have gone over to the TNC camp and are also helping the TNCs shackle the unions. Still, if enough of us mobilized our power as citi-zens, consumers and workers, we might still prevail.

Before that can happen, however, a lot more people will have to understand that Canada is not being restructured by forces beyond their control, but by the CEOs of the Fortune 500.

To laugh that off as a leftist conspiracy theory is to emu-late the skeptical cow in the cartoon.

Not that we'll suffer the same bovine fate. We won't be-come hamburgers.

Just hamburger-flippers.❖

The corporate cancer

After reading Richard Preston's best-selling book *The Hot Zone*, no one would conclude that the deadly Ebola virus strains are involved in a conspiracy to destroy the human species.

They are just doing what comes naturally. Given a chance to get inside a human being, they'll keep multiplying until they kill their host—even if that means ultimately destroying themselves. That's what viruses do. It's their nature.

Cancer cells don't conspire, either. They don't get together and plot how they're going to ravage your lungs or your breasts or your prostate. They just do what they're genetically made to do.

It's the same with corporations and banks. They're not engaged in a conspiracy to rule the world. They don't gather monthly to plot the wholesale destruction of jobs, families and communities. That's just an unfortunate side-effect of their obsession with profits and power.

In our glorious free enterprise system, business executives are programmed to maximize profits without regard for the society in which they operate, in much the same way that virus or cancer cells are programmed to proliferate without regard for the health of their host.

That's why, in writing about the anti-social behaviour of corporations, I've never accused them of being involved in a conspiracy. They're behaving exactly as the capitalist ethos directs them to behave in the absence of effective inhibitors. To accuse them of a conspiracy would make no more sense than accusing beavers of conspiring to build dams in order to flood nearby farmers' fields; or accusing termites of plotting to wreck your house.

There's one big difference, however, between these biological analogies and the activities of transnational corporations. It is this: We do everything we can to protect ourselves from cancer and viral infections, and to be cured if they get through our defences. We relocate or cull the beavers if they become too destructive. And we call in the exterminators as soon as we find evidence of termites in our homes.

In sharp contrast, we are doing virtually nothing to curb business depredations. We excuse and rationalize layoffs, plant shutdowns and relocations, the export of jobs to low-wage countries, corporate tax avoidance, industrial pollution, obscenely high CEO pay and perks, even the business take-over of our political system. All the ill-effects on people, we tell ourselves, are unavoidable. Free enterprise would not be free if companies were not allowed to do these things.

The high-priests of capitalism are fond of their own biological comparison. It's "the law of the jungle." Nature, they remind us, has divided the animals into predators and prey. It's the nature of predators (corporations) to prey on the rest of us. The lion, after all, must get the largest share. As the king of the beasts, that's his right and privilege.

As an allegory, however, this invocation of the law of the jungle is badly flawed. The lion may indeed get the largest share, but he doesn't take *more* than his share. He doesn't keep on killing antelopes and other animals simply for the joy of killing. He takes just enough prey to meet the immediate needs of himself and his family. You don't see lions piling up carcases out of greed, or hoarding food that's needed by smaller creatures.

The true law of the jungle is that there is a balance among all life-forms, in which they all have a place and a share. Nature usually provides checks to stop one species from seriously harming others. (Humankind has been the exception, so far, although nature may soon have something nasty like the Ebola virus to put an end to our planetary vandalism.) Within the global economic system, however, the outbreak of an unrestrained form of capitalism, spread through the new communications technologies, threatens the survival of human civilization.

CEOs and their apologists will no doubt resent their being compared with runaway cancer cells, but I think the simile is an apt one. Let's not forget that, a hundred years ago, unfettered free enterprise caused so much misery and squalor that it had to be forcibly humanized. Laws were passed to make companies conform to minimal social standards. Their conduct was regulated. Their profits were taxed. Strong unions emerged to force them to stop mistreating their workers, to pay them adequately, and provide them with safe working conditions.

The corporate "cancer" was thus controlled. In fact, properly harnessed and regulated, its growth proved to be relatively benign, giving us in the three decades after World War II what now can be looked back upon as "a golden age." But it always remained a cancer, and, freed from constraint, would behave like one—as we now, to our dismay, have learned.

One by one, the anti-cancer curbs have been removed. Regulations have been scrapped. Governments have been turned into company annexes. Unions have been weakened. National boundaries have been wiped out.

Free to spread through human society virtually unhindered, with no checks or balances left, the corporate cancer is doing what comes naturally to all cancers. It is growing. It is maximizing its assets. It is feeding on its hosts, who unfortunately happen to be the 90% of us who make less than $100,000 a year. Eventually, of course, the other 10%—the favoured overclass—will also succumb, since capitalism does require some vestige of social stability to survive.

But that's not a consideration of today's CEOs, who don't look any further ahead than the next quarter's financial statement. That's a lack of foresight they share with cancer cells, which also lack any real intelligence.

Whether any serious effort can or will be made to re-regulate the corporate viruses (or strengthen our social immune-system against them) is the key question for the 21st century. The only point I wanted to make here is that I don't believe that the members of the Business Council on National Issues, the Canadian Manufacturers' Association, the Chamber of Commerce, or any other business group are part of a diabolical conspiracy.

They're just doing what corporations naturally do when they are given absolute dominion over our economic lives. Like any efficient cancer, they set about consuming their hosts.❖

Free trade fiasco

Almost unnoticed, Jan. 1, 1998 marked the 10th anniversary of the Canada-U.S. Free Trade Agreement, which was later expanded and renamed the North American Free Trade Agreement (NAFTA). NAFTA, in turn, is slated to be the model for a much broader free trade agreement spanning North and South America, to be completed by 2005.

The insistent claim of business and political leaders is that free trade has been good for Canada. It has been credited with keeping inflation down, expanding trade, increasing cross-border investment, and making our industries more competitive. Without free trade, they contend, unemployment would be even higher, recessions worse, and public spending cuts even deeper.

The pro-free-traders conveniently ignore the many negative developments of the past 10 years—the exodus of manufacturing plants and jobs to the United States and Mexico, the sharp decline of real income and purchasing power, the conversion of millions of permanent and well-paid jobs to precarious low-wage, part-time and contract employment, the ever-widening chasm between rich and poor, the shocking rise of both poverty and homelessness, the deterioration of our health care, education, welfare, and other social programs.

It is now obvious to all but the most extreme right-wing ideologues that the free trade deals were a key component of a neo-liberal policy agenda that, since the 1970s, has been ravaging national economies and rolling back the post-war gains of working people. Privatization, deregulation, monetary austerity, public sector cutbacks, investment and trade liberalization—these and other elements of the corporate agenda have indeed freed the markets; but they have combined to make life more difficult and insecure for most Canadians.

The rationale of the corporations is that free trade is essential to make them more competitive. The drumbeat of "competitiveness" is at the heart of the NAFTA dynamic that has so gravely affected employment and income. To that end, corporations have been freed to downsize, relocate, extort wage and other concessions from unions. Capital has been freed to move wherever it can find the lowest wages, taxes and environmental safeguards. Workers, on the other hand, have had their rights and freedoms correspondingly curtailed, as have Canadians generally in their roles as citizens, consumers and voters.

NAFTA has made it easier for Canada's business barons and their political allies to bring about the "structural adjustment" of our social and labour institutions in line with the dominant U.S. model. Thanks to NAFTA, what had previously been a purely domestic U.S. policy agenda has been extended to Canada and Mexico. Entrenching these pro-business, anti-people policies in a formal treaty has provided insurance against backsliding by future politicians, strengthened the rights of investors, reined in interventionist governments, and seriously reduced the rights and powers of organized labour.

By the 10th anniversary of its implementation, free trade had clearly fallen far short of its promise to improve general prosperity and economic stability. On the contrary, NAFTA is tearing apart the social and economic fabric of Canada—and arguably of the United States and Mexico, too.

Activists in countries all through the Americas are now working together in an effort to prevent this destructive model from being imposed on the people of Central and South America. If successful, it could serve as the impetus for a much-needed campaign to relieve the people of Canada, the U.S. and Mexico of the free trade yoke that has hobbled and handicapped them so disastrously for the past 12 years.❖

Free trade: still the No. 1 concern

The CCPA's monthly journal, *The CCPA Monitor,* runs a few free-trade-related articles in almost every issue, which some readers seem to think is a waste of space. They're the ones who believe that, since we failed to avert the passage of the FTA and NAFTA, the free trade battle is over, we lost, so we should move on to other worthwhile struggles. Like protecting the environment. Like preserving Medicare and other social programs. Like resisting the attack on unions' rights.

What these let's-give-up-on-free-trade proponents don't seem to realize is that, as long as the free trade deals remain in effect (in their present form), they will make it virtually impossible to win the other battles. All the social, economic

and environmental problems we face, from poverty to pollution, from unemployment to the underfunding of health care,
are linked in some way to free trade.

This is because the free trade deals are charters of rights
and freedoms for corporations. Their underlying intent is to
free corporations from all restraints on their operations, to
enable them to pursue the maximization of profits without
interference from governments, unions, or any other organization.

Combined with deregulation and the conversion of all
governments to the corporate agenda, free trade enshrines
corporations as the unchallenged rulers of the global economy.
The trouble is that what's good for General Motors, or any
other corporation, is no longer good for most people (if, indeed, it ever was).

The corporations prefer low wages, low taxes, low environmental standards. They resent having to pay even a small
share of the cost of health care, education, unemployment
benefits, pensions, or other social programs. They like high
unemployment. They like low wages. They like weaker unions. They detest Greenpeace and other environmental
groups. They are quite prepared to tolerate high levels of
poverty and pollution if the alternative is for them to pay fair
wages and taxes or spend more on curbing toxic emissions.

The upshot is that all of the individual campaigns by individual unions, community-based coalitions, anti-poverty
or pro-equality groups are basically campaigns against the
abuse of corporate power. That corporate power may be exercised through the legislative actions of compliant governments (and thus shrouded from public view), but there should
be no doubt who our real enemies are.

Nor should there be any doubt about the source of the
corporate power that bedevils us in so many ways. The source
of their power is free trade. It is free trade that enables them

to shift jobs to low-wage countries, free trade that lets them thumb their noses at national needs and boundaries, free trade that puts their interests above everyone else's.

Those on the left who dismiss free trade as a lost fight or a dead issue—who are content with token "side deals" on labour, human rights and the environment—tend to portray themselves as pragmatists or realists. But in fact it is they, not those who continue to attack free trade, who are being naive and impractical. To accept free trade, while still trying to oppose its separate social and economic consequences, is surely the ultimate in naiveté.

There's no denying the difficulties involved in striving to have NAFTA revoked, or extensively revamped. Nor in confronting the WTO, the FTAA and APEC. The forces arrayed against us are immensely powerful—but they are not invincible. All over the world, people are coming together to challenge corporate rule, and that means, first and foremost, dismantling the free trade regimes that give corporate rule its sanction and legitimacy.

To abandon the campaign against free trade is therefore unthinkable. On the contrary, it must continue to be the overarching objective of all our struggles for social and economic justice.❖

Bread and circuses

The Roman emperors had a two-fold formula for preventing popular uprisings: bread and circuses. They figured that people who were well fed and entertained would be reasonably content and disinclined to revolt. And most of the time they were right. A full belly and a good seat in the arena to watch the gladiatorial fights took most people's minds off their rulers' despotism and debauchery.

It's safe to assume that today's rulers also rely on a modern version of the bread-and-circuses recipe to keep people tranquilized. Providing bread is no problem. Even those without jobs can escape starvation with the help of welfare payments and food banks. But what are the modern equivalents of the Roman circus?

Most of us might think that television, movies and sporting events serve that diversionary purpose, but I think there is a much more insidious opiate—the political process itself. Our governments don't provide the entertainment. They *are* the entertainment.

In ancient Rome, you see, the politicians were also the plutocrats—the owners of most of the land, slaves and wealth. The emperor and the senators exercised economic as well as political power. The laws and decisions they made originated with them. They were not being manipulated by powerful interests "behind the throne."

In Canada today, we are also ruled by plutocrats, but they are *not* the politicians. Our rulers are the unelected and unaccountable corporate executives, bankers and money traders who now set the political agenda for all governments of all stripes. Prime ministers and premiers do their bidding. The policies favoured and the laws enacted are those that enhance the wealth and power of the plutocracy. (It's no coincidence, surely, that the chief beneficiaries of the Liberal government's high interest rates in the 1990s—the banks and investment firms—were also the most generous contributors to the Liberal party. The banker doesn't live who's willing to part with a dollar without expecting to get at least $10 back, in one form or another.)

Canada's political system, thus subverted, has become little more than a puppet show. The politicians posture and pontificate, actors on the parliamentary stage, following the script written for them by the Business Council on National

Issues. Their debates, their hearings, their consultations, their press conferences are as carefully choreographed as professional wrestling matches—and as meaningless.

Unfortunately, while most people know that wrestling matches are a form of amusement, they haven't yet come to realize that the political system has fallen into the same category. Even the Press Gallery journalists continue to write and talk about what the politicians are doing as if the politicians' antics really do belong on the front page instead of in the entertainment section.

The real power-wielders in their executive suites benefit enormously from this kind of theatrical politics. They can count on the media to cover political developments as if they really mattered. They can count on citizens who are unhappy with their government to blame the government instead of the government's overseers. They can count on dissident groups wasting their time lobbying and haranguing the politicians, in the mistaken belief that it is the politicians they elect who are running the country.

I would go so far as to argue that all those who continue to importune the politicians are unwittingly helping to legitimize the charade that now passes for democracy in Canada. The protesters, too, are dancing on the business barons' puppet-strings, acting out their role as dissidents on the elaborate political stage. If they are free to march and demonstrate, you see, the system must be democratic.

Indeed? The reality, of course, is that the politicians will not respond—will not be *permitted* to respond—to such vulgar displays by the underclass. Our governments now govern solely on behalf of the 10% of the population who comprise the ruling class. They are subservient to the corporate executives who have supplied the funding and media propaganda for their electoral victories.

Such governments are held on a short leash. They are not "in power" because they have no power. The laws they pass and the policies they adopt are dictated by the plutocrats who have hijacked our political system—and, with few exceptions, these laws and policies are confined to those that benefit the rich and powerful.

As long as people continue to demonstrate in front of the legislative assemblies instead of the business towers, as long as they occupy the offices of cabinet ministers instead of corporate boardrooms, as long as they blame the puppets instead of the puppeteers, the modern political "circus" will serve its intended purpose.

It will divert people's attention from their real problems, and their real enemies. It will focus their anger and frustration against the servants of the plutocrats, instead of the plutocrats themselves. It will strengthen people's simplistic belief that working through the electoral system and favouring one gang of political "wrestlers" over the others is still the only way to bring about needed changes and reforms.

Canadians thus beguiled are not much different from the ancient Roman plebians who neglected their civic duties to watch the gladiators fight.

The only difference that I can see between the Roman circuses and our parliamentary circuses is that some of the gladiators really did get killed.❖

"Money is like manure"

"Money is like manure, not good except it be spread," Sir Francis Bacon observed over 400 years ago. If he were alive today, he would be appalled by the extent to which money is *not* being spread. Increasingly, it is accumulating by the billions in the bank vaults and accounts of an affluent minority.

This is the inevitable result of the revival of laissez-faire capitalism, and the unbridled greed it has unleashed. In such a survival-of-the-fittest economy, the smartest and most ruthless among us are bound to grab disproportionately large shares of the national (and international) wealth.

The proponents and defenders of this system see nothing wrong with such an unfair distribution of income. It's the way a truly free market works, they proclaim. They have all the assurance of religious fanatics. Their market god can do no wrong.

Many critics of this barbaric business dogma, including me, have called for the infusion of some moral or ethical principles. But this is like appealing to the clemency of Attila the Hun—and with about the same results. Morality to the corporate high priests is an alien concept. They will never be swayed by calls for decency or fair play. Like the Grinch's heart, their collective conscience has atrophied.

So the only effective way to make a case for a more balanced distribution of income is to argue that it would strengthen, not weaken, the private enterprise system. Leaving aside the whole debate over the ecological limits of growth, this is basically the argument for raising and expanding the consumption of private sector goods and services. In a system that depends as much on demand as on supply, it makes no sense to concentrate solely on the supply side. A glut of unsold products leads to declining profits and rising bankruptcies. Economics 101.

You'd think that would be so self-evident that even the stupidest CEO would favour the widest distribution of income. Instead, our brightest business leaders prefer high unemployment and poverty, falling real wages, and cuts in government social assistance—all of which sharply reduce disposable income.

Then they wonder—duh!—why people aren't spending more: why they aren't buying new cars and furniture, why they aren't attending as many hockey games or rock concerts.

It's important, however, to differentiate between the global corporations which are no longer dependent on domestic consumption, and the less fortunate small and medium-sized business firms that are. If you look at the corporations that are raking in record profits, you see that nearly all of them are in the export sector. It's our exporters whose business is booming, because by definition their sales are made outside the country. They are not affected when Canadians have less to spend. Their customers are the well-heeled élites in the growing economies of Southeast Asia.

Apart from the exporters, the only domestic firms that are impervious to the maldistribution of income are the banks and the other big financial and investment houses. The banks couldn't care less if their annual $6 billion profits are derived from six million people depositing $1,000 each or from 1,000 people depositing six million dollars each. Either way, they get the same amount of money.

The smaller businesses that do rely on volume purchases are not so lucky. For them, the prolonged drop in consumer spending has been critical, and for many disastrous. You would think that at least some of these Canadian-based retailers and merchants—like Eaton's, for example—might have figured out before it was too late that their interests are not the same as those of the big global corporations—that, on the contrary, they are diametrically opposed. But so far they have remained oblivious. They continue to support the downsizing, the wage cuts and freezes, the reductions in UI and other public programs, as enthusiastically as their larger business colleagues.

"We want people to have less to spend," they are in effect saying, "but we still want them to spend more."

No wonder so many of these dummies are going belly-up.

Eventually, the growing concentration of wealth in fewer and fewer hands may catch up with the TNCs, too. There's a limit to how many cars and computers they are going to be able to sell in a world where the bottom four-fifths of the population have barely enough to stay alive.

To dramatize the underlying instability of laissez-faire capitalism, researchers at Simon Fraser University recently decided to "shrink" the Earth's population to a village of 100, with the relative size of human groups and incomes remaining the same. They found that, in such a global village, six people would have half the world's wealth, 50 would suffer from malnutrition, and 80 would have to live in substandard housing.

Now, obviously a village with that kind of grotesque income disparities would not last very long. Even if it could, how would an entrepreneur get a successful business going? He/she would need to sell more than six shirts or rugs or hamburgers—or haircuts or theatre tickets—to make even a meagre profit.

Even if the six rich people hired a dozen of the less well-heeled to protect them from the penurious (and resentful) majority, a revolution of some sort would eventually bring the whole unjust system crashing down.

On a global scale, however, the same social and economic inequities can be maintained for a longer period. The world's poorest people are mostly confined to Africa, Latin America and parts of Asia, far from the secluded estates of the wealthy élite. They are not needed as consumers, at least not yet. Four out of five of the world's people have annual per capita incomes of less than $1,000. They can't even afford to buy a telephone, let alone a TV set or a computer, or get credit from a bank—and yet the biggest electronics firms and banks keep piling up record profits.

This is because the one-fifth of income earners at the top are still numerous enough—they comprise more than a billion people, after all—to provide the purchasing power needed to keep the global economy working. At least for the big transnationals.

But what William Greider calls "the manic logic of global capitalism" is pushing growing numbers of businesses—the ones dependent on sustained levels of domestic consumption—over the brink.

The TNCs shrug off these casualties. In a system based on the survival of the fittest, they aren't surprised that the "unfit" don't survive. Perhaps they even envisage a future in which the new corporate Darwinism will leave just a hundred or so giant super-corporations straddling the globe and controlling its economy.

Greider, however—whose most recent book *One World, Ready or Not* I highly recommend—predicts that the gross inequities and social disruptions spawned by global capitalism will inflict such "wrenching calamities" on the world's countries and people that the system will ultimately crash.

He doubts whether business and political leaders will heed the warning signals in time to avert such a collapse. "The global system so dominates and intimidates present thinking," he writes, "that I expect societies will be taught still more painful lessons before they find the will to act."

The proof of his pessimism—or is it optimism?—can be found in the blindness of the free-enterprisers to the iron law of income distribution. If the geniuses who now drive the free market system can't even see what Bacon saw 400 years ago—the basic need to spread the money—they can hardly be expected to stop their mad rush toward ultimate self-destruction.❖

How the IMF started
the war in Kosovo

One of the problems with figuring out that corporations now rule the world is that you tend to get dismissed as a crazy conspiracy theorist. So, even though I knew the International Monetary Fund (IMF) had sowed the seeds of the 1999 conflict in the Balkans, I hesitated to point an accusing finger at this particular agent of the corporate agenda.

It was a relief, therefore, when the finger-pointing was done by Bob Allen, a respected economist and historian at the University of British Columbia. In his CCPA study *Why Kosovo? Anatomy of a Needless War*, Prof. Allen traced the roots of the outbreak over Kosovo directly to the IMF.

Granted, the deep hostility between the Serbs, the Croatians and the Albanians fuelled the mass killings of the past few years, just as it did countless other massacres during the past four centuries. The enmity between these ethnic groups has been passed down from generation to generation and is always simmering. But it can be kept in check, as Yugoslav President Tito effectively demonstrated.

Tito, of course, ruled as an absolute dictator from the end of World War II until his death in 1980, and it's tempting to assume that it was his iron hand that kept the Serbs, Croatians and Albanians from each other's throats during his long reign. No doubt the fear of Tito was a factor, but police state methods alone would not have preserved ethnic peace. A much more effective policy was the provision of a relatively high level of social and economic security during the Tito years.

Yugoslavians did not enjoy what we regard as democracy under Tito, but the country's unique system of labour-managed industries and market socialism provided them with good jobs and excellent health care and education programs.

This sense of security and well-being, more than Tito's dictatorial powers, accounted for the abeyance of ethnic strife. People are much less likely to vent age-old antagonisms if they are all well-fed and living in comfort.

Tito's demise, however, opened the door to Western corporations, banks, and the IMF. The familiar pattern of rising foreign debt, high interest rates, and the inevitable debt repayment crisis so prevalent among Third World countries now came to devastate Yugoslavia's economy. The government appealed to the IMF and World Bank for assistance, and of course it was granted—but only on condition that the country undertake the "reforms" that comprise the typical IMF structural adjustment program.

Freed from the dictatorship of Tito, Yugoslavians now had to bow to the dictatorship of the IMF. (I leave it to you to decide which of the two forms of tyranny they would prefer today.)

The conditions imposed by the IMF included a wage freeze, high interest rates, the privatization of all labour-run firms as well as the banking system, and the deregulation of financial transactions and foreign trade.

As you might expect, these IMF-enforced policies combined to wreck Yugoslavia's economy. Plant closings and layoffs multiplied, unemployment soared, social programs were cut. Government spending was drastically reduced, and all transfers to the republics and autonomous regions (including Kosovo) were diverted instead to the repayment of foreign debt.

One of the immediate consequences was to undermine the republics' allegiance to the central government in Belgrade. Kosovo, in particular, with its majority of Albanians, was the hardest hit by the IMF reforms and the quickest to rebel against them. Its growing army of jobless young people provided most of the recruits for the newly-formed Kosovo

Liberation Army. Ethnic tensions, suppressed under Tito, were re-ignited.

Probably the single event that contributed most to the Kosovo uprising was the decision of Milosevic's government to revoke Kosovo's autonomy in 1989. This move was condemned by the United States and Canada as an act of aggression against the Albanian majority in Kosovo, but in fact (as Prof. Allen makes clear), it was yet another result of the IMF dictates.

The IMF insisted that its "reforms" be implemented in all regions of the country, including Kosovo. But, as long as it remained autonomous, Kosovo could and did reject them. So the only way Belgrade could meet the IMF's demands was by removing the region's autonomy and making it once again subservient to the central government.

Of course, for the Albanians in Kosovo this was the crowning insult, and over the next several years it led to the atrocities committed by both sides of the conflict, to the refugee crisis, and ultimately to the NATO bombing rampage.

The important thing to remember about this whole outburst of violence is not so much that it was a direct result of IMF policies, but that these policies have been devised to benefit the privileged and powerful few who now run the global economy.

These are the architects and enforcers of corporate rule, through the IMF, the World Bank, the WTO and APEC, and the blood on their hands is by no means confined to the Balkans. Their ruthless reallocation of the world's wealth and resources from the poor to the rich, at any cost, has spread unemployment, poverty, suffering and death around the world on a scale never seen before in human history.❖

PART II

Corporate Rule: Maintained

Why complain? The UN says we're No. 1!
The charge of the Left Brigade
Our leaking lifeboat
Waiting for the trickle
Money: The ultimate weapon
The New World Order: Here to stay?
Grim thoughts on entering the new millennium

Why complain?
The UN says we're No. 1!

On the day after the United Nations—for the fourth year in a row—declared Canada to be the best country in the world in which to live, I scanned the morning papers to find out what was happening in this most idyllic of all places on Earth. Surely, I thought, the *Ottawa Citizen*, the *Globe and Mail*, and the *Toronto Star* would be chock full of cheerful, positive, constructive, optimistic, comforting, fulfilling news about our earthly paradise.

No conflicts to report here, surely. No unhappiness, no poverty, no inequality, no adversity. Not in the country rated No. 1 four years in a row.

Well, let's look at the headlines.

"Ontario Tories to fingerprint welfare recipients, force single parents to work for their benefits." Workfare? In paradise? Obviously a misprint.

"No more federal money for poor children for two more years, says Chrétien, or until the deficit is eliminated." Hmm. The bankers and other money-lenders must be in greater need than the million-and-a-half kids whose parents' incomes fall below the poverty line.

"Unions angry about suspension of bargaining rights." I guess you can't please the unions anywhere, not even in Utopia.

"Markets soar to record highs." Well, at last, a story about happy, affluent Canadians, for whom our top UN ranking is clearly justified.

Some of you may question the UN's methods of assessing a country's quality of life. You may find it odd, for example, that the ratings ignore the distribution of income *within* a country. What the UN does is divide the total wealth by the number of citizens, which in Canada's case produces a per capita figure of over $21,000. That's pretty high. It gives a family of four—any family of four—an annual income of nearly $85,000.

You may object that this is not the real Canada. You may even say that it's a never-never land that exists only in the UN's Human Development Index. You may point out that, even if the population of Canada consisted of, say, 100,000 multi-millionaires and 29 million paupers, the UN would still rate us near the top in per capita income and quality of life. True, but what's wrong with that? Figures don't lie, especially those generated by the UN.

If you are one of the whiners and ingrates who don't appreciate our No. 1 UN status, you might also question our high ranking in educational attainment. Granted, you might say, nearly all of us get to go to school, and most of us graduate, and many of us even get through university. But a diploma or a degree isn't much good to someone who can't find a job.

You conveniently forget that employment is not one of the UN's criteria. Whether someone has a job or not has no connection with a country's quality of life, as measured by the UN. Neither, for that matter, does poverty. Oh, yes, the UN did chide our federal and provincial governments, ever so gently, about their indifference to child poverty and youth unemployment, both among the highest in the industrialized world. But these slight defects are completely offset by our world-class life expectancies.

Canadians on average live slightly longer than their counterparts in Norway, the No. 3 country, so, even though Norway has virtually no poverty and an unemployment rate of less than 4%, its quality of life trails behind ours on the UN index. You may doubt that most of our jobless and homeless would agree that living longer is preferable to living better, but, hey, who are we to argue with the UN?

Many countries in Europe also have much more generous social programs than Canada's—especially since the sharp funding cuts of the past five or six years. But again, to the UN, superior health care, higher unemployment benefits, bigger pensions, better day care, stronger environmental protection laws—none of these social standards really matter. Not enough, at any rate, to be factored into its Human Development Index.

That makes Canada No. 1. The best place on the planet to live. So don't complain about our millions of poor and unemployed, about our hungry kids, about the dismantling of our social benefits, about our regional and gender inequalities, about our unfair tax system, about the yawning gulf between the rich and the rest of us. What counts is that we live longer, stay in school longer, and (mathematically, at least) have higher per capita incomes.

Having achieved such near-perfection, we should be content to sit back and enjoy life in this Canadian Eden. Let the politicians continue to coddle us. Let the corporations keep lavishing us with high-paying permanent jobs. Get rid of the unions and other "special interest" troublemakers like the CCPA and the Council of Canadians and Greenpeace and the anti-poverty and pro-equality groups. Who needs them any more, now that we're so securely ensconced at the top of the global living quality heap?

If these grumblers and malcontents don't appreciate living in this veritable heaven-on-earth, then let them move to Norway or France, which, as Nos. 3 and 4, are still struggling to catch up with us. Ha! Let's see how they like living in countries where the life expectancy is a month or two less! Oh, sure, maybe they'll find it easier to get work, and maybe their actual pay will be higher, and maybe they'll get better health care and pensions and child care and so on, but we'll have the last laugh. We'll still be alive for a couple of months after they're gone!

So let's give thanks to the UN for its annual tribute to this most fortunate and felicitous of nations. It serves to tighten the grip of the big corporations on our economy. It validates the exploitation of our resources and the pollution of our environment. It consolidates the political reign of right-wing politicians. It accelerates the dismantling of our social programs. It justifies the deregulation of our service industries and the sell-off of our public assets.

Some stubborn and short-sighted Canadians see these developments as undesirable, even harmful. But if the result is to give us the best country in the world in which to live, surely we should stop being so negative.

The UN, after all, was created more than 50 years ago to create international harmony, to put an end to wars, to eradicate poverty and hunger and homelessness and illiteracy. In view of its outstanding success in pursuing all these objectives, who could quibble with its Human Development Index? If the UN says Canada is No. 1, then by God, it must be true, and all evidence to the contrary must be mere illusion.❖

The charge of the Left Brigade

George Bernard Shaw used to tell the story of how he encountered "the man who lost his keys."

Walking home from a theatre one night, he came upon a man on his hands and knees under a lamp-post, obviously searching for something.

"I've lost my keys," the man told Shaw.

The playwright joined in the search, but after several minutes it was apparent the keys were nowhere to be found.

"Are you sure you lost your keys here?" Shaw asked him.

"Oh, no, I lost them in that dark alley over there," the man replied, "but it's a lot easier to look for them out here in the lamp-light."

I am reminded of that anecdote every time I see angry protestors milling about in front of government buildings, every time I hear a speaker at the mike raging against government legislation, every time I hear or read of non-government agencies submitting briefs or petitions to committees of politicians.

It is indeed a lot easier to look for the "keys" to a more just and caring society in the brightly-lit legislative chambers than in the secluded boardrooms of corporate power. But it's a search that is just as futile as that of Shaw's man under the lamp-post.

Canada has been under corporate rule for the past 20 years. All our governments since the late 1970s, federal and provincial, have been committed to implementing the corporate agenda, most willingly, others through intimidation. The pretense of democracy has been maintained, but the reality is that all governments have taken—and continue to take—their votes from Main Street and their orders from Bay Street.

During these two decades, all the groups and individuals who wanted to preserve the relatively benign and progressive society of the post-war golden age have protested the relentless wave of cutbacks, privatization, deregulation and free trade. But they've done so by appealing to the politicians who implemented these destructive policies on behalf of their corporate masters.

Whole forests have been felled to provide the paper for the thousands of briefs that have been presented to parliamentary committees, and the mountains of letters, faxes and petitions that have been sent to the corporations' political stooges. The telephone wires have been clogged with angry phone calls to MPs and MLAs. The lawns in front of the legislatures have been trampled by hordes of noisy demonstrators.

All these "charges of the Left Brigade" have been to no avail. The politicians pay no heed to those who are victimized by the laws and policies they implement to make the rich richer and the powerful more powerful. Occasionally, yes, to preserve the illusion of democracy, the political wrecking crews may introduce a harsher measure than their corporate overseers demand so that it can later be reduced to the level actually desired. This lets the leaders of the protesting groups claim a spurious "victory," but the implementation of the corporate agenda is never significantly retarded.

There is an urgent need to restore true democracy in Canada. On that point I agree with the unions, the environmentalists, the anti-poverty groups, and others that truly represent the public interest. Where I disagree profoundly with them is that this can be done in the misguided and clearly ineffectual ways that have failed so miserably for the past 20 years.

You simply cannot overthrow corporate rule by protesting against and pleading with the political agents of corporate rule. To continue pursuing such a sterile strategy is inadvertently to help consolidate corporate rule, not expose or challenge it.

The pretense that lobbying, protesting and demonstrating against the corporations' political flunkeys will ever have the slightest effect on the corporations themselves does a grave disservice to the great majority of Canadians. It sends them a completely false message. It tells them that it is the politicians, not the CEOs, who are to blame for the dismantling of Canadian society. It tells them that democracy is still alive and well in Canada and that all they have to do to improve their lives is to write or phone their MPs, or join yet another demonstration.

If only one-tenth of all the time, energy and talent that have been wasted on such political protests could have been directed at the real enemies of Canada; if only a small bit of that prodigious but foredoomed effort could have been devoted to exposing and challenging our corporate rulers—we would all be a lot better off today.

If we keep on targeting the political puppets and ignoring the corporate puppeteers, I can envisage the protesters trudging down from Parliament Hill in the year 2020, congratulating one another that their lobbying against the Liberal-Progressive government's Child Labour Bill has had the desired effect.

"Without our efforts, the bill would have allowed corporations to hire children below the age of eight, instead of age ten."

"Yes, it was a great victory. Almost as great as our campaign last year to prevent the minimum wage from being lowered to $1 an hour instead of $2."

"We're on a roll. Our next campaign to limit floggings in the workfare camps to 20 lashes instead of 25 also has a good chance of succeeding."

"All these victories sure do prove how worthwhile it is to channel our protests through the political process. It's a good thing we didn't listen to poor old Ed Finn when he wanted us to tackle the corporations instead. Think of where Canada would be today if we had!" ❖

Our leaking lifeboat

The Chrétien government's craven surrender to the Ethyl Corporation came as no surprise to those of us who know that governments now cater solely to corporate interests. We were surprised when the Liberals banned the importation of Ethyl's toxic MMT gasoline additive, but we knew they'd have to back down after the company laid a NAFTA complaint.

The Liberals knew that, too, or should have (assuming they'd read the NAFTA text before signing it). They were aware that, from then on, they couldn't protect Canadians from industrial chemicals—not without forking over massive amounts of taxpayers' money to compensate a company for lost profits, legal costs, and alleged damage to its reputation.

The 1997 ban was therefore a meaningless gesture, designed to make the Liberals look good to environmentalists just before an election. The $20 million they had to give Ethyl a year later could be written off as a deferred election expense.

The whole episode was just another symptom of the disease of globalization that now afflicts the whole planet. With governments converted into business lapdogs, there are no organizations left to protect the public from corporate greed. The planet's resources have been offered on a platter to the TNCs to exploit as they wish, its ecological systems left defenceless against their depredations.

Given the dependence of all the Earth's inhabitants—even the wealthy élite—on the planet's basic life-support capacity, you might think that even the most selfish and powerful CEOs and stock market speculators would by now have started to have doubts about the infallibility of their "free market" doctrine.

And a few of them are indeed having such qualms, including Wall Street financier George Soros, the U.S. Republican party's Pat Buchanan, former U.K. Thatcher cabinet minister John Gray, and even the chief economist of the World Bank, Joseph Stiglitz.

They are now saying, in effect, that free trade was a mistake, and so is the unrestricted flow of capital. But their dissent from the prevailing business-knows-best ideology is not being taken seriously. They are dismissed by their right-wing associates as mavericks or even traitors. And so the global corporate plunder continues, and to hell with the social, economic and environmental consequences.

The current situation could be compared with that of people stranded 100 miles from shore in a large but leaking lifeboat. The leaky stern of the boat, partly submerged, is occupied by the third-class passengers, who are up to their waists in water. (Let's call them the workers.) The second-class passengers are a little better off, the water being only up to their ankles. (Let's call them the middle-managers.)

The most fortunate, so far, are those in first class, who are still snug and dry in the uplifted bow-section. They also are the only ones with guns, so they have taken most of the food and blankets for themselves. (Let's call them the CEOs.) They care nothing for their fellow passengers, especially the workers at the stern, who are getting so weak they can no longer do the tasks they've been assigned, which are bailing out the water and pulling on the oars.

The mid-managers are better treated, if only because they stand between the workers and the CEOs. They are given a small share of the food, enough to keep them from starving, but are expected to replace any workers who collapse and can't keep bailing and rowing.

Now, if the CEOs at the dry end of the boat weren't blinded by their ideology and upper-class status—if they had even a modicum of intelligence—they would see that their comfort and safety could not be sustained at the expense of their fellow passengers. They would understand that the sensible thing to do would be to have all the passengers working together, cooperatively, to keep the boat afloat while they rowed to dry land. They would share the food and blankets equally, would have everyone (including themselves) taking turns bailing and rowing. That way, they would all have a chance of surviving.

But these CEOs are so used to giving orders, to living in luxury, to treating their workers as inferiors, that they can no longer change their ways. Their ideology is stronger even than their sense of self-preservation.

So they continue to maintain in the lifeboat a society that mirrors that of the broader global economy—one based on greed, power and privilege, not on cooperation. They leave it to the workers in the sinking end to do all the bailing and rowing, with a bit of help from the middle managers. When a worker collapses, they have him or her thrown overboard to lighten the loan and delay the inevitable foundering.

When all the workers have drowned or starved to death, the middle-managers are forced to replace them, but by now so much of the boat is submerged that no amount of bailing can save it, and rowing any distance is impossible.

Most of the CEOs, however, are still dry and well-fed and complacent. And so it comes as an awful shock to them when the boat finally takes its fatal plunge. How could this happen to them? Hadn't they done exactly what the New World Order decreed? Hadn't they won the no-holds-barred race to amass the most wealth and power? How could the poverty and sickness and misery of the lower classes have had such a devastating effect on them, the élite of the human species?

And so they go to their watery graves, still unaware that the passengers in a leaky lifeboat can't be divided into winners and losers. Either they all win, or they all lose. It's as simple as that.

Our planet is our lifeboat. And the planet, too, is "leaking." Its water and air are being contaminated, its forested areas destroyed, much of its arable land eroded, many of its animal, plant and insect species wiped out.

The minority who grow rich from pillaging the environment and impoverishing billions of their fellow human beings are indifferent to the dangerously detrimental effects on the planet itself. They live in palatial and well-guarded estates, far away from their victims, untouched as yet by the crop failures, the droughts, the storms, the smog, and the other environmental "leaks" that already afflict billions of the less fortunate around the globe.

Will the wealthy financiers, investors and CEOs who now occupy the still "dry" bow of our planetary lifeboat come to realize their folly and self-destructiveness before it's too late? Will they curb their avarice—or have it curbed for them by those they exploit—in time to reverse and repair the ecological damage already done?

If not, if the élite don't soon smarten up, the future that looms ahead of us couldn't be gloomier. The 21st century, in that case, may well be the one in which our destructive and suicidal human race engineers its own well-deserved extinction.❖

Waiting for the trickle

"The economy is doing fine, the people aren't," General Emilio Medici, former military dictator of Brazil, calmly admitted in the early 1970s. He could afford to be frank. His brutal regime made no pretense of serving "the people," catering openly and exclusively to the country's business élite.

The only difference between Medici and the political and business leaders of Canada today is that the latter still pretend to serve the people. They welcome the growth in GDP, extol the rise in corporate profits, hail the booming stock market, praise the surging export sector. All signs of a strong and healthy economy, they tell us.

We are supposed to feel good about these developments, even if we're not among the affluent few investors who benefit from them.

The reality for most Canadians is one of stagnant or even falling incomes, job insecurity, and a shredded social safety net. For many of us, unemployment, perhaps even poverty, are only a few pay-cheques away.

Not to worry. As the economy keeps expanding, some of its rewards will eventually trickle down to everyone. At least, that's what our leaders soothingly reassure us.

This trickle-down promise has never been kept in the past, and is even more hollow today; yet a surprisingly large number of people still swallow it.

Perhaps it's not all that surprising. Modern economics—or, more precisely, the dominant free-market version of economics—has taken on all the trappings of a religion. And, as in any religion, its basic principles and pronouncements must be accepted as articles of faith, regardless of how much they diverge from reality and reason.

Anything that doesn't correspond with the religion of laissez-faire capitalism—high levels of unemployment and poverty, for example—must therefore be rationalized as temporary aberrations, accepted as normal and natural, or blamed on enemies of the true faith, such as trade unions or other heretical "special interest groups."

In an essay in "Z" magazine, Edward S. Herman explains how "the economics of the rich has been re-established as the core of mainstream economics." Most economists, he says, now identify completely with the ruling corporate élite and preach and defend the economic theories that favour this élite. They have in effect become the free-market religion's high priests.

Similarly, the media have become the business religion's propagandists. They are, after all, owned by big business, get most of their revenue from business advertisements, and most of their senior editors, columnists and reporters are also members of the ruling class.

"The media gravitate naturally toward economists who speak élite 'truths' that the media understand and favour," says Herman. "These economists are also given credibility as 'experts' by their affiliation with corporate-funded think tanks. The rare think tanks that offer dissident ideas, most notably the Economic Policy Institute [and the CCPA in Canada], are labelled 'labour-backed' by the media and used sparingly." The think tanks that get nearly all their funding from business, on the other hand, are never called "corporate-backed," and are quoted extensively.

The world-wide spread of private enterprise and its dogma in the 1990s has been aided and accelerated by the collapse of communism in the Soviet Union and Eastern Europe. Communism was the chief rival of capitalism, ideologically as well as economically. Its abandonment by the Russian empire left capitalism as the only "workable" economic system, the only one allegedly deserving of our unequivocal support, if not worship.

Unbridled and unchallenged capitalism, however, is as much a threat to true democracy and prosperity as communism ever was. The reason communism failed was not because it was implemented by dictators, but because it was based on the false premise that the state alone can meet people's economic as well as social needs.

Capitalism is by no means incompatible with tyranny. Indeed, corporations seem to prefer dealing with dictators, judging by their very profitable operations in Indonesia, Burma, and other countries ruled by military juntas. Dictators tend to be even more indifferent to corporate excesses than democratically-elected governments. The use of child labour, pollution of the environment, and the pillaging of natural resources are much easier when they are not only tolerated, but actively encouraged.

Russia and its satellite nations, however, allowed no room at all for private enterprise. Governments tried to have everything done by or through the public sector, including the production of cars, washing machines and toothpaste. Naturally this system broke down. There are some things that governments shouldn't do, and can never do well.

At the same time, there are some things that corporations shouldn't try to do, such as provide essential public services. It was not capitalism that triumphed, but rather the mixed economies of the West in which both the public and private sectors played the roles most suited to them. Governments looked after people's social needs, while corporations met their consumer needs.

The private enterprise fanatics, however, were never happy with this arrangement. They have always wanted to shrink the responsibilities of government and take over all its activities that could generate a profit.

The collapse of communism gave them the opportunity to discredit government everywhere. "See, this is what happens," they crowed, "when governments get too big and bureaucratic. They become incompetent and wasteful—unlike business firms, which are always efficient and cost-effective."

This specious claim has now been simplified and reduced to a "government-bad-business-good" mantra. The less government the better. Cut government spending. Reduce government programs. Privatize government institutions. Contract out government services. Let business run the country as it should be run.

These are not statements of fact, because they cannot be validated. They are canons of faith in the catechism of the new global corporate religion, and are thus not open to question.

Those who do dare to differ are easily dismissed as heretics and heathens, as fools or troublemakers. Even when the dominant business orthodoxy is publicly questioned by a respected member of the establishment, such as Henry Mintzberg, a professor of business management at McGill, such dissenting views are given scant attention and quickly buried.

Prof. Mintzberg, in an essay published in the prestigious *Harvard Business Review*, argued that government and business both have a place in a well-balanced economy. "I do not wish to receive my policing services from General Motors," he wrote, "any more than I wish to buy my cars from the government.

"Attacks on government," he added, "are attacks on the fabric of society. We have individual needs, to be sure, but a society that allows them to undermine collective needs will soon destroy itself."

His warning went unheeded, of course, as do all views that don't conform with the theology of global capitalism.

In the old Soviet Union, all critiques of the communist creed were also suppressed. We have seen the disastrous consequences when government usurped the role of business. The result of business usurping the role of government will be even more disastrous.❖

Money: The ultimate weapon

When Magna CEO Frank Stronach recently rephrased the Golden Rule to mean "He who has the gold makes the rules," he could have been referring to the International Monetary Fund (IMF) and the World Bank.

Most Canadians have heard about these two agencies, but few are aware of the awesome scope and severity of the "reforms" they have imposed on nearly every developing country in the world. So overwhelming is the power they wield on behalf of the world's large corporations and financial institutions that the cumulative effect has been to create a global plutocracy. It's a new world order in which those with the gold indeed make the rules, and—through the IMF and World Bank—ruthlessly enforce them.

In his recent eye-opening book, *The Globalization of Poverty: Impacts of IMF and World Bank Reforms*, Michel Chossudovsky, a professor of economics at the University of Ottawa, doesn't mince words when he tells us how the IMF and World Bank accomplished this world-wide coup d'état.

The "structural adjustment programs" (SAPs) imposed on more than 100 indebted countries in the Third World and Eastern Europe, he says, amount to a form of "market colonialism [that has] led to the impoverishment of hundreds of millions of people" and the ruination of many countries' economies.

"The globalization of poverty in the late 20th century is unprecedented in world history. The poverty is not, however, the consequence of a 'scarcity' of human and material resources. Rather, it is the result of a system of global oversupply predicated on unemployment and the worlwide minimization of labour costs."

The two Washington-based bureaucracies have been directed by international creditors and trans-national corporations (TNCs) to execute "a global economic design which affects the livelihood of more than 80% of the world's population:

"Internal purchasing power has collapsed, famines have erupted, health clinics and schools have been closed down, hundreds of millions of children have been denied the right to primary education...The reforms have been conducive to a resurgence of infectious diseases, including tuberculosis, malaria and cholera...The process of deforestation and the destruction of the natural environment [has led] to the forced displacement and eviction of several million people."

Chossudovsky goes so far as to call these SAPs "economic genocide" in that they deny developing countries any possibility of building national economies that would serve their own citizens. Instead, most of the Third World has been turned into "reserves" of cheap labour and natural resources to be exploited by the TNCs.

Inevitably, in many countries thus ravaged, famines and epidemics break out, as do social, racial and regional conflicts. The role of the IMF and World Bank in triggering these disasters is never admitted or reported, but Chossudovsky pins the blame where it belongs. In the second half of his book, he describes in detailed case studies how IMF and/or World Bank interventions precipitated the most recent famine in Somalia, the genocide in Rwanda, the military coup in Bangladesh, the economic destruction of Vietnam, the civil war in Yugoslavia, and the development of the illegal drug economy in Bolivia.

In other case studies, he relates the horrendous effects of the IMF's "shock treatment" on the people of India, Brazil and Peru, and tells how the IMF engineered the "Thirdworldization" of the post-cold-war Russian Federation.

The Western industrialized nations, of course, have also been subjugated by the financial powers, though not directly through the IMF and World Bank. Instead, free trade, capital mobility, and the adoption of neoliberal economic policies similar to the SAPs have had the same effect of putting the TNCs in charge.

Where the advanced countries have been directly affected by the IMF and World Bank is in the development of cheap-labour export factories in the Third World. As Chossudovsky points out, the result has been plant closures and mass layoffs in the Western nations, and "the impact on real earnings and employment has been devastating."

And with high unemployment and stagnant or falling wages comes an inevitable decline of consumption.

"It's a vicious circle: the relocation of industry to the South and the East leads to economic dislocation and unemployment in the developed countries, which in turn tends to push the world economy into global recession...The global economic system is thus characterized by two contradictory forces: the consolidation of a global cheap-labour economy on the one hand, and the search for new consumer markets on the other. The former undermines the latter."

Chossudovsky doesn't think the new world order created by the IMF, the World Bank and the TNCs is here to stay. He says the global financial system is "highly unstable" and is only kept going by what he calls the rise of "luxury consumption." The increased concentration of income and wealth in the hands of privileged minorities in most countries has led to "the dynamic growth of the luxury-goods economy: travel and leisure, the automobile, the electronics and telecommunications revolution, etc."

But Chossudovsky warns that this provides, at best, only a temporary "breathing space" to a global economy beset by recession.

"The world community should recognize the failure of the dominant neoliberal system," he says, and take steps to reform and humanize "this global economic system based on the relentless accumulation of private wealth."

He admits there are no "technical solutions" to this crisis, and calls on social movements all over the world to come together "in a common pursuit and commitment" to bring to an end "the massive concentration of financial wealth and the command over real resources by a social minority."

This is a struggle, of course, that is already well under way by social activists in many countries, whose combined efforts recently scored a major victory in the campaign against the MAI. Their ongoing struggle will be immensely strengthened by Chossudovsky's informative study. This is the most effective exposé yet written about the IMF's and World Bank's brutal "reforms" and their role in spreading and deepening poverty around the world.❖

The New World Order: Here to stay?

The big question now is whether the newly globalized capitalist system is consolidating its supremacy, or whether it is careening out of control and doomed to self-destruction.

Those wishful thinkers who favour the latter scenario are not impressed by the awesome and unchallenged power now wielded by the transnational corporations (TNCs). They argue that any machine lacking both internal and external controls will eventually be impossible to operate. If its gears and pinions accelerate beyond a tolerable limit, it runs the risk of tearing itself apart.

The basic instability of unfettered capitalism, they say, is that it is activated solely by greed. And greed unleashed can lead to horrendous social upheaval. Up to the mid-1970s, that greed was held in check by democratic national governments and strong unions. Legislated regulations and negotiated labour contracts forced Big Business to share its profits on some minimally equitable basis with workers, consumers, and the state.

Over the past 25 years, all these external constraints have been thrown off. Globalization, free trade, deregulation, the new communications technologies, and the conversion of nearly all political parties to the free market agenda have combined to subvert governments and disempower unions. Nothing has since stood in the way of corporate domination. In a frighteningly short time, it has spread around the globe, causing poverty and joblessness on a massive scale.

There have been signs recently of some uneasiness among the corporate élite. They fret about the continuing drop in consumer spending. The festering social malaise makes them nervous. So do the street protests by workers in some countries. Some CEOs have even publicly voiced concerns about a possible backlash against their downsizing.

But these expressions of disquietude by our corporate rulers are still very much exceptional. Most of them remain confident that "the market" must and will prevail, and that any socioeconomic problems spawned by their profiteering are either temporary or manageable.

If they're right, globalization early in the 21st century will create a feudal world ruled by the kings and queens of commerce, with their courtiers and hangers-on, living in luxury in their modern palaces, wallowing in nine-tenths of the world's wealth. The survival of the financially fittest will be ensured, while the vast majority of people are mired in poverty and serfdom.

Most Canadians can't envisage such a brutal and inequitable system being set up without opposition—or without crashing first from its own excesses. Even if it could be, they would not see it being sustainable for very long. Surely, they reason, if the masses of people were so abused and exploited, they would rise up against their oppressors.

I wish I could share that optimism. But I think a new corporate feudalism could indeed be established, and in fact is already in the process of being established. It may even be achieved without any effective resistance, and could possibly last for hundreds of years, just as its feudal precursor prevailed during the Middle Ages.

This is because our corporate overlords have mastered the propaganda apparatus that has convinced the masses to acquiesce in their own subjection. If most people are persuaded that the New World Order and all its adverse effects are being caused by natural and unstoppable forces, they will not try to defend themselves. If they can be convinced that the law of the jungle is the right and proper law to govern human activity, they will fight among themselves instead of against the economic jungle's powerful predators.

During the Middle Ages, it was the Church that provided the "propaganda" needed to keep the serfs resigned to their misery. Told by their bishops and priests that the aristocrats were ordained by God to rule over them and that they would be rewarded in the "next life" for their suffering in this one, they remained docile for centuries.

Today, it's the corporate-controlled media that preach the inevitability—even the desirability—of the new global feudalism. Newspaper editors and columnists, radio and TV commentators and talk-show hosts, academic pundits and right-wing apologists play the role of high priests in this Malthusian free-market religion. It is their function to delude the victims of globalization into thinking it is futile (even sinful) to try to oppose it.

"It's your own fault," they're told, "that you are among the many losers instead of the few winners in the global economy. If you worked harder, became more ruthless and competitive, you too could join the ruling class."

This insidious message, endlessly repeated, erodes the will to resist. Encouraged to squabble among themselves for their corporate rulers' leftover scraps, the majority of people fall easy prey to this sort of mental manipulation. If their brainwashing can be maintained, it is indeed possible that a global corporate empire (The Fourth Reich?) can be created that will endure for generations—or until the environment is irreversibly devastated—and without the need for legions of armed guards or other overt forms of oppression. After a generation or two, even the most deprived and mistreated of serfs tend to accept their lowly state without a murmur.

There are only three ways to avert the creation of such a corporate feudal system.

The first is to have a reimposition of the constraints that formerly kept private enterprise within relatively civilized bounds. This in turn, however, would require the politicians to defy their corporate masters, and therefore must be considered highly improbable. (It is made even more daunting now by the globalized scope of corporate power, which effectively rules out such an initiative by any individual country. It would take all the G7 countries acting in concert—at the very least—and what are the chances of that happening? Zilch.)

The second way to stop the corporate juggernaut would be for the TNCs themselves to voluntarily pull back from the goal of absolute global dominion, even though it is clearly within their grasp. This will happen only if they doubt their ability to avert or overcome possible opposition and to keep the system from self-destructing. Although such doubts have been expressed, it seems that most CEOs remain committed to their global strategy. (In any case, it would be necessary for all the big TNCs in each industrial sector to agree jointly to limit their profit-seeking—for all the corporate lions, in other words, to become lambs. So scratch that option, too.)

The third and last way to forestall the Global Corporate Empire is therefore the only one that is practically achieveable. It consists of an all-out effort by the individuals and organizations that oppose the TNCs to de-brainwash their fellow citizens—to expose the corporate agenda, refute its inevitability, and show that there are better and viable alternatives to the New World Order.

There's no guarantee, of course, that, even if most people are thus enlightened, their new awareness will translate into a mass rejection of the corporate agenda. But one thing is certain: as long as they remain the mental prisoners of that agenda, they will never resist it or even question it.

What is required is a massive education and communications campaign, conducted on many fronts. It would not be easy to mount. It would be expensive. It would require a lot of effort by a lot of people. It would be hampered by its limited access to the commercial print and broadcast media. But it could be accomplished if those with the resources and the decision-making authority decide it should become their No. 1 priority.

Whether the leaders of the left will undertake such a major effort to wage and win the propaganda war is problematical. It is much easier for them to mobilize their minority of activists for useless marches and demonstrations. It is much easier for them to posture and pontificate at conventions, or to rely on a political process that is now under corporate control. It would be much more difficult—and offer far fewer photo-ops—to concentrate on changing public opinion. (Or even to edify the 90% of their own members who have also been indoctrinated by the right-wing propagandists.)

It would be tragic enough if corporate rule were to become entrenched despite the strongest efforts to challenge it. Even more tragic would be a failure to lose the struggle because the opponents of corporate rule fought against it with the wrong weapons. Time is running out. The only effectual weapons are the facts, figures and arguments that discredit the corporate agenda. If they—and the means of disseminating them—continue to rust while the left wastes time and money organizing marches on the Parliament Hill servants' quarters, the New World Order is here to stay.❖

Grim thoughs on entering the new millennium

Starting a new millennium, it's a good time to think about the future of the human species. It's a time to ask ourselves, objectively, whether we can count on surviving for another millennium. Or for another century. Or even for another few decades.

As the world's most renowned scientists warned us eight years ago, "The Earth is finite. Its ability to absorb wastes is finite. Its ability to provide food and energy is finite...And we are fast approaching many of the Earth's limits. Current economic practices ...cannot be continued without the risk that vital global systems will be damaged beyond repair."

Although this urgent exhortation in 1992 came from eminent scientists in 70 countries, including over 100 Nobel Prize winners, it was ignored at the time (not even reported by the mainstream media!) and has been ignored ever since.

Granted, we've had several summit-level conferences on climate and the environment, including the one in Rio de Janiero in 1992 and the one at Kyoto, Japan, in 1997. And glib promises were made at these meetings to reduce carbon dioxide and other greenhouse gas emissions. But, as with most promises made by politicians, they were promptly reneged on when the delegates returned home. All of the environmentally destructive practices that the scientists warned us about have been continued, and many have even been intensified.

Now, you have to wonder about this rush toward self-destruction. Why do we keep befouling our planetary home? Why do we risk making the Earth uninhabitable? Is there some lemming-like death wish buried deep in our genetic makeup? Are we, as a species, collectively insane?

As individuals, few of us knowingly want to commit suicide. As individuals, we don't want our children and their children to live (or die) in a global cesspool. As individuals, we profess to be very concerned about the contamination of our air and water. As individuals, we recycle our rubbish, we join and support Greenpeace, we sign petitions imploring our political leaders to give environmental issues a higher priority.

As a species, however, it's a different story. We support an economic system that glorifies greed and unrestrained consumption. We tolerate an unfair distribution of income that dooms billions of people to poverty and disease. We buy and drive cars and trucks that poison the atmosphere. We dump raw sewage into the lakes and rivers. We clear-cut forests and exterminate other forms of life.

Ultimately, all these practices harm every one of us.

It's interesting to compare humankind as a species with other creatures that Nature has experimented with over the eons. Ants and beetles and bees and termites are among the most successful, having been around for countless millennia. They've survived, I would say, not just because they've adapted so well to their environment, but because their most basic instinct is to put the welfare of the collective—the ant-hill or the hive or the nest—ahead of personal well-being. An individual ant may lack intelligence, as we define it, but the ant colony is arguably a model of enlightened self-interest.

Among the larger animals, Nature's most effective creations were the dinosaurs. They were the dominant life-form on the planet for many millions of years, and probably still would be today if a gigantic asteroid hadn't slammed into the Earth and caused disastrous climatic changes that wiped them out. They certainly didn't self-destruct, as we seem intent on doing, because they did nothing to despoil or damage their environment.

It may well be that Nature's mistake in experimenting with humans was to make us intelligent as individuals, but monumentally irrational as a species. There's a lot to be said for individualism; none of us would prefer the conformity of the anthill; but when individualism is elevated into the prevailing economic ideology, as it has been with capitalism, then we get into deep trouble. Why? Because what's considered good for us as individuals in the short term is suicidal for us as a species in the long term.

What we have done is to cede all decision-making power to those who benefit the most from the most reckless and ruthless individualism. The world's affluent minority of billionaires, stock-holders, bankers, money traders, investors and CEOs now run the global economy. They are motivated solely by greed and the power that their prodigious capital assets bestow on them. They are committed to the unlimited exploitation of the planet's resources, to the unlimited production and consumption of non-essential junk, to the unlimited accumulation of personal wealth.

And, oh, yes, they exert control over all governments and virtually all political parties. Their purchased or intimidated politicians can now be counted on to serve the narrow interests of their corporate masters, not those of the great majority of citizens.

Consider, as an example, what really would have to be done to reduce the major source of greenhouse gas: the emissions from motor vehicles. Far fewer cars and trucks would have to be operated, and far fewer roads and highways built. But that would drastically reduce the profits of the oil companies, the auto-makers, and the road construction companies, all of whom wield vast political as well as economic power. Can you seriously imagine that any government would dare antagonize such prominent business leaders— and generous political campaign contributors?

Another example is the weapons-of-war industry. The production and sale of arms that kill people—and, incidentally, add enormously to global pollution—is another multi-billion-dollar business, and the companies and military forces that specialize in this gruesome activity are also so large and powerful that no government dare challenge them. Again, it is worth asking whether a species that spends much more on hurting its members than helping them can lay any legitimate claim to sanity.

Some observers (including venerable economist John Kenneth Galbraith) still believe the greatest threat to human survival is an outbreak of nuclear war, and they could be right. We may well bomb ourselves into extinction before we have time to asphyxiate ourselves with toxic pollutants.

Am I being unreasonably pessimistic? I sincerely hope so, but I fear I am only being pragmatic. The enshrinement of greed, individualism and competition as the driving forces of the global economy pushes us ever closer to the brink of doom.

With politicians and the mass media having been co-opted as allies of the corporate anti-life movement, where are our potential saviours? The environmentalists? The labour unions? The churches? The NGOs that oppose free trade and globalization? I suppose that, if they could all come together and pool their resources, they might stand some chance of rescuing us; but unfortunately that doesn't seem a likely prospect.

We are left, it seems, with one slim hope: that some horrendous and highly visible sign of our planetary depredations will occur that will shock us into a more rational outlook. It seemed for a while that global warming might do the trick, but this is such a gradual process that it could conveniently be ignored, and has been.

We've all heard the allegory of the frog in the pot. Dropped into a pot full of hot water, the frog will quickly jump out. But placed in a pot of lukewarm water that is slowly heated, the frog stays in and is eventually boiled.

Today we are the human equivalents of that frog. Our environment is being degraded, but so slowly that our instinct of self-preservation is not activated. It will probably take a major disaster—the melting of the Antarctic ice-caps, perhaps, or a planet-wide drought—to jolt us into taking self-protective measures. (Such as overthrowing our corporate rulers and replacing them with leaders committed to a sane and sustainable economy.)

Whether such a drastic wake-up call comes in time to ensure our survival as a species is of course problematical. The scientists who issued their warning in 1992 estimated we had only about two decades from then—till 2012—to launch the needed reforms.

Twelve years into the new millennium is an alarmingly short time to regain our sanity as a species. But if we fail, we join the dinosaurs—not as the helpless victims of a climate change caused by an asteroid, as they were, but as the victims of our own collective stupidity.❖

PART III

Corporate Rule: The Myths

What we "know" that ain't so
The money is there
Scapegoating the poor
Wealth and charity
Fantasy and reality
The "good" old days

What we "know" that ain't so

"It's not what we don't know that hurts us. It's what we know that ain't so."
— Will Rogers.

Most Canadians are relatively well-informed. There's not much they "know" that ain't so—except when it comes to the country's economy. On that subject they've been very cunningly and cynically misinformed. Unfortunately, it's these deeply-instilled economic myths that are hurting them the most.

Nowhere is this more evident than in the public acceptance of—even support for—massive government cutbacks. According to a recent poll, most Canadians want the government to continue to cut the federal debt rather than try to create jobs and rebuild our shattered social programs.

The Liberals, of course, like other political Neanderthals, argue that this can only be achieved by spending less—even though such cutbacks cause more unemployment, lower incomes, less consumer spending, and less tax revenue.

Abraham Lincoln used to say that democracy was safe because "you can't fool all of the people all of the time;" and even with the perfection of modern propaganda techniques that's still true. (After all, one-third of Canadians have seen through the neo-liberal nonsense.)

All it takes, however, to dismantle the welfare state, keep interest rates higher than they should be, privatize Crown corporations, underfund health care and education, deprive two million people of jobs, relocate industries to low-wage Third World countries, deregulate business, lavish tax breaks on the wealthy, and have the second highest level of child poverty in the developed world (second only to the U.S.)—

all it takes to create such an unjust society is to fool most of the people most of the time.

This is the function of the right's indoctrination experts. Having unlimited access to the media, they keep saying that all these harmful effects of the corporate agenda are necessary to ensure Canada's competitiveness in the harsh global economy. "There is no alternative, folks," they tell us glibly.

The effectiveness of this "big lie" is reflected, as well, in a recent Angus Reid poll of young Canadians, those between the ages of 16 and 25. This is the generation that is being hurt the most by government and corporate downsizing, and the dearth of jobs. But do they disapprove of the right-wing policies that are depriving them of hope for a decent future? Not at all. Most of them—nearly 70%—actually applaud the cuts in public spending, and want them to continue!

It's not that they're masochists. They have simply swallowed the prevailing twin falsehoods: 1) that the public debt is the cause of all their problems; and 2) that this debt was caused by government overspending.

The facts, of course, are that almost all the public debt was piled up because of excessively high interest rates, excessively high unemployment, and an excessively unfair tax system that favours profitable corporations and wealthy individuals. Only about 6% of the increase in government debt since 1984 can be attributed to government spending on our social programs, which, even before the cuts of the past decade, were far less generous than those of the more enlightened countries of continental Europe.

These facts can be substantiated by anyone who takes the trouble to check them. So can the fact that the right-wing prescription for economic growth—public sector cuts and corporate downsizing—weakens the economy instead of strengthening it.

A recent study in the United States disclosed that all six economic depressions in that country's history were preceded by attempts to balance government budgets. "The record shows that deficits have never triggered depressions," Frederick Thayer noted in *The Washington Spectator,* "whereas crusades to reduce the national debt have always been followed by depressions."

The lesson of the last Great Depression in the 1930s is that spending cuts only serve to perpetuate the social and economic devastation. That depression, like all the previous ones, was ended only when government spending was increased, when more jobs were created, when the tax system was used to redistribute income toward the people most likely to spend it on goods and services.

Those policies are very much in disfavour these days—so much so that anyone daring to espouse them risks being ridiculed or branded a crackpot. "These guys are living on the moon," sneered Tom d'Aquino, president of the prestigious Business Council on National Issues, in dismissing the economic stimulus proposals of the CCPA.

Many Canadians—maybe as many as 25% of them—don't share d'Aquino's derogatory view of the CCPA. They have open minds. They refuse to be brainwashed. They would prefer to examine the centre's alternative policies before passing judgment on them.

If enough additional Canadians were to do that—and it wouldn't involve a trip to the moon, or even to Ottawa—future polls might indicate a long-overdue majority rejection of the neo-Victorian New World Order.❖

The money is there

Whenever one of us "bleeding-heart liberals" complains about the deep cuts to health care, education, welfare, unemployment insurance, and other social programs, we get a scolding from the corporate and political downsizers.

"You're living in the past," we're told sternly. "The time has gone when governments could afford to keep funding such a strong and generous welfare state. The money just isn't there any more."

Most Canadians glumly accept this claim as one of the hard realities of the 1990s. In fact, it is sheer tommyrot. There is more money in our economy today—a lot more—than there was back in Canada's "golden age" in the 1960s and early 1970s.

Go back 28 years to 1972, when our social programs were at their peak. Canada's per capita Gross Domestic Product that year (in constant 1986 dollars) was $13,617. By 1995 our per capita GDP (also in '86 dollars) had soared to $20,558. That's an increase of more than 50%—and by now that increase has undoubtedly climbed to at least 60%.

So we now have a country that is far richer than it was in 1972, in terms of the total money the economy generates, but one that somehow allegedly can't afford to maintain the basic social programs we managed to fund without any difficulty in the 1960s and 1970s with far less national income.

Somehow there's not enough money today to prevent 20% of our citizens—nearly one-and-a-half million of them children—from falling into poverty. Not enough money to create jobs for 8% of our work force. Not enough money to pay decent wages to the people fortunate to still have jobs.

What we clearly have, in reality, is a manufactured shortage of funds for these social purposes. A manipulated shortage. A sleight-of-hand shortage.

There is more money than ever, but it has been redistributed in a way that drastically cuts the amounts available for government spending on programs and services. Instead of being at the disposal of governments to serve the general population, it is being diverted into the overflowing coffers of the country's business, financial and social élites.

How was this massive transfer of money from the public sector treasury to the private sector purse accomplished? Very smoothly and cunningly. So cunningly that most Canadians still don't realize what has happened. They don't understand that the country's financial "crisis" was deliberately engineered.

The strategy for reducing the federal government's disposable revenue had several components.

The first and most effective was to massively increase the federal debt. The more indebted the government, the more it would have to borrow, the more it borrowed the higher would be its deficits, and the less it would have left to fund social programs.

This particular ploy was pioneered by the Reagan government in the United States in the 1980s, at the behest of its corporate overlords, and has been described in detail by Reagan's director of the Office of Management and Budget, David Stockman. He has admitted publicly that the sole intent of piling up that country's federal debt was to provide an excuse to cut social spending—and to prevent successive governments from reversing the program cuts.

To force his government into borrowing more, Reagan gave huge tax breaks to business and wealthy individuals, thus draining billions from tax revenue. Then he had the U.S. central bank, the Federal Reserve, raise interest rates to record levels, allegedly to fight inflation. The real reasons, of course, were to increase the cost of government borrowing, while at the same time pleasing the banks, the money traders, and the media and academic neo-cons.

Excessive interest rates had their intended effect of sending the economy into a tailspin, leading to the layoff of millions of workers, who in turn stopped paying taxes, as did the thousands of small companies that went bankrupt or failed to make profits.

It wasn't long before the Mulroney government in Canada adopted the same strategy. Tax breaks to business and high income earners have skewed our tax system, too—so much so that more than 80,000 profitable companies now get off completely tax-free, and the rest are taxed at a fraction of the rate imposed on Canadian workers.

The Bank of Canada went on the same anti-inflation crusade as its U.S. counterpart, and with the same results: record-high interest rates, mass layoffs, a sharp drop in government tax revenue from the newly unemployed, and a concurrent steep rise in UI and welfare outlays.

To plunge Canada even deeper into the hole financially, our central bank also steadily reduced its share of the federal government debt (on which the government of course pays no interest) from nearly 20% to 5%, inviting the private banks to move in and make the loans instead. This substantially raised Ottawa's debt payment charges and further reduced the amounts available for social spending.

These contrived shortfalls provided the excuse needed to increase government borrowing, while the insanely high interest rates added enormously to both the debt and the cost of repaying it. Once heavily indebted, the politicians could claim (falsely, but all too plausibly) that it was overspending on "too generous" social programs that had caused the financial crisis. They had no alternative, they told gullible voters, than to cut back on health care, education, UI, and welfare spending.

The induced debt/deficit hysteria has served the neo-con politicians and their business masters better than they had hoped. It has permitted them to gut with impunity the public programs and services that benefit the majority of Canadians. It has enabled them to divert billions of dollars from wage-earners into the overstuffed vaults of the bankers and other money-lenders. It has provided the rationale for dismantling and wrecking the public sector, selling off Crown corporations at bargain-basement prices to the corporate predators. It has recreated the market-driven survival-of-the-fittest society of the Victorian era, in which the rich get richer, the poor poorer, and the middle class smaller.

Canadians have so far swallowed the myth that all the misery and poverty and insecurity inflicted on them could not be avoided. They can't help noticing, however, that the banks and the big corporations are reaping record profits, that billions of dollars change hands daily in the stock markets, that big business executives enjoy million-dollar salaries and bonuses, that the Cadillac and Mercedes-Benz dealers can't keep up with the demand for their luxury cars.

Maybe they will soon make the connection between this lavish private sector and the impoverished public sector. Maybe they will start to wonder if there really is a money shortage.

Maybe they will even come to believe that the next politician or CEO who tells them we can no longer afford our social programs is being somewhat less than truthful.

The truth, as any X-Files fan will attest, is out there.

So is the money.❖

Scapegoating the poor

Observing the barrage of anger, resentment and hate now being hurled against people on welfare, I'm reminded of the old African proverb: "As the waterhole gets smaller, the animals get meaner."

As the basic resources diminish, in other words, so does the willingness to share. So do the qualities of tolerance and neighbourliness. The sense of community is replaced by an ugly survival-of-the-fittest mentality.

There is, however, a big difference between what happens at a shrinking waterhole in Africa and what happens in Canada when jobs disappear, incomes stagnate, and government services are cut back. The waterhole gets smaller because there's a drought. It's a natural and unavoidable phenomenon. In Canada, however, the necessities of life for the weakest among us are being deliberately and needlessly withdrawn.

Our welfare "waterhole" is being siphoned away, its contents diverted from the pockets of the poor into the stock portfolios of the rich. There is no shortage of money in Canada. Business and bank profits soar to dizzying heights. Corporate executives and speculators wallow in wealth. But they will not be satisfied as long as a cent remains to be squeezed out of their lowest-income victims. A mere one-and-a-half million children going to bed hungry every night? Not nearly enough. Corporate Canada's sights are set on a much higher number.

In the past, picking on the weak and the poor was not normally something that the business élite and their political flunkeys could do with impunity. Prior to the Nasty Nineties, most people would be shocked by all this welfare-mom bashing. Even the most hardened right-wingers would at least raise their eyebrows. Today, however, as food is snatched out of the mouths of hungry kids, the writers of letters to the editor and the hot-line radio show callers enthusiastically applaud.

The media, instead of describing the plight of the thousands doomed to destitution, maliciously search for and expose the few people on welfare who are abusing the system.

Although they are the exceptions, they are depicted as typical "welfare bums," too lazy to work and living comfortably and parasitically off the hard work of others.

It's surprisingly easy to stir up this kind of hatred of the underprivileged. The human animals indeed get meaner as their economic waterhole gets smaller. They don't blame the bloated plutocrats who are greedily sucking up most of the country's fluid assets. They turn their fury on the most wretched and disadvantaged members of society—those at the very bottom of the income ladder.

It's eerily reminiscent of a laboratory experiment in which sadistic scientists provoke naturally peaceful mice or guinea pigs to fight among themselves. This is done with an extended family or colony of mice that coexist in harmony as long as they all have enough to eat and drink. Gradually the scientists start reducing their supply of food and water. They want to find out at what reduced level of sustenance the mice can be induced to "compete" for their dwindling rations.

Eventually hunger turns the biggest and strongest mice against the weaker ones. At first they simply nip at them and drive them from the food containers. Then, if the food is drastically curtailed, the attacks become fiercer. Carried to its extreme, this experiment results in the death of the weakest mice, either from their wounds or starvation. A cooperative and democratic community is deliberately converted into a war zone.

Like these lab mice, we Canadians are being subjected to a steady reduction in our means of livelihood. Our business rulers are forcing us to make do with fewer jobs, lower incomes, declining services, pared-down unemployment insurance, less reliable health care, and a shredded social security net.

Being somewhat more intelligent than mice or guinea pigs, we didn't have to react as they did. We could have directed our anger against our corporate and political tormentors instead of attacking our less fortunate fellow citizens. When we scapegoat the poor, the jobless and the homeless among us, we are allowing ourselves to be manipulated. We are letting the corporate lab technicians trigger our most brutal and sub-human instincts.

Our unemployment and poverty rates are now among the worst in the industrialized world. Fourteen countries have a more generous UI system than we do. We rank 47th—far behind even Third World countries—in the gap between our men's and women's earnings. We spend considerably less on our social programs, as a percentage of GDP, than do most countries in Europe.

Our economic and social waterhole, in short, is getting smaller—is being coldly and callously *made* smaller.

So far we have responded predictably by getting meaner. It's time we got smarter.❖

Wealth and charity

Media mogul Ted Turner's $1 billion donation to the United Nations to help alleviate world poverty was warmly applauded. As it should have been. But what motivated him to part with all that cash? Was it pure altruism? Was it guilt for amassing that huge amount in just nine months on the stock market? Or was it insurance against a populist revolt by the millions denied such affluence?

I pose these questions because I've always wondered how the world's billionaires and multi-millionaires live with themselves. With very few exceptions, they haven't really earned their wealth—or they've "earned" it by exploiting and mistreating their fellow human beings. Unless you win a lottery, that's just about the only way to accumulate millions in an economic system that glorifies greed.

Anyone with above-average intelligence, a particular talent, and a wide streak of ruthlessness can claw his or her way up the income ladder. Many thousands have done it. But how they can then look at themselves in the mirror every morning is what I have trouble comprehending.

I probably could have joined the ranks of the affluent myself, if I wasn't bothered by a conscience. I was only in my early 30s when I became managing editor of a daily newspaper. I hob-nobbed with publishers and other senior editors. I wasn't making a lavish salary then, but I'm sure I could have risen well into the six-figure bracket by the time I reached middle age, had I stuck with the newspaper business.

I didn't because I was gifted with (some would say hobbled by) an active conscience. When my publisher ordered me to report only the employer's side of a major labour dispute, I resigned instead of complying. Had I been willing to abandon my principles, not to mention my adherence to journalistic fairness, I would no doubt have made my first big step up the corporate hierarchy and to larger pay-cheques, bonuses and stock options.

Instead, I decided to go to work for the labour movement, and spent the next 32 years editing and writing for union publications. But I don't want to appear to be taking a holier-than-thou attitude. I literally could not have made any other choice and still have preserved a shred of self-respect. In any case, what I may have lost in monetary terms was more than offset by the opportunity to put whatever skills I had to the service of working people. (And don't get me wrong: the unions always paid me enough to maintain a decent living standard.)

The labour dispute that caused me to change careers was the 1959 loggers' strike in Newfoundland. The strike was broken by the intervention of Premier Joey Smallwood on the side of the paper companies. Up to that time, Joey had been a champion of workers and their rights, and had even worked as a union organizer before getting into politics. After Joey sold out to the companies and decertified the union, the late great Toronto Star cartoonist Duncan MacPherson depicted him sitting on a throne above which an inscription read: "Better to rule with management than serve with labour."

Joey somehow managed to live with himself after his switch in allegiance, but I think I was a lot happier with my move in the other direction—to serving with labour instead of ruling with management.

The paper company moguls seemed happy, too, after the strike was broken, because they could keep on paying the loggers a few dollars an hour, forcing them to sleep on boughs in drafty shacks, feeding them bread and baloney at almost every meal, and denying them proper safety equipment to reduce a horrendous toll of lost limbs and lives.

Today's CEOs, major shareholders and speculators seem equally indifferent to the appalling human misery on which their fortunes are built. They pay workers as little as they can, deny them adequate benefits and job security, and dispose of them when they're no longer needed. Child and prison labour in the Third World is harnessed to their drive for profits. Anti-unionism, deals with dictators, attacks on social programs, pillaging resources and polluting the environment— no method is considered unacceptable as long as it boosts profits, dividends, and CEO pay packages.

Some of these corporate monsters have no moral or ethical scruples whatsoever. Either they were born without them, or they've managed to suppress or deactivate them in some way. The others, however, need some way to rationalize or even exalt their cutthroat behaviour in order to retain some modicum of self-esteem.

A few of them do it the Rockefeller-Carnegie-Turner way, by allocating some part of their wealth to charitable causes.

This feeds their egos and reduces their taxes, as well as assuaging any feelings of guilt about their money-making tactics.

Other plutocrats are so ideologically wedded to the capitalist system that they are able to overlook its flaws. They've convinced themselves they're rich because they deserve to be, because that's their reward for being more competitive and innovative and energetic than the lazy bums on welfare.

Then there are those among the financial élite who truly believe that a system based on the survival of the fittest is the only workable way to conduct business. It's a reflection of nature, they say. They are the predators, and it's their nature to prey on the weak and those handicapped by moral principles.

Basically, the rich see nothing wrong with the wide disparities of income that have opened up between them and the "lower" classes. Given a choice between living in opulent luxury and trying to make ends meet on a typical worker's budget, they would consider it stupid to forfeit their privileged position. And not only stupid, but unjustified, no matter how their wealth was piled up.

Those who have some scruples left may regret the poverty and misery that afflict most of the world's people. They may seek to overcome these misgivings through charitable donations and activities, as Ted Turner has done. But none would go so far as to favour putting limits on the amounts of wealth any individual or family could accumulate, or taxing back a good deal of it, so that charity would no longer be needed. That (horrors!) would be socialism, or even communism.

The billionaires' self-respect is not threatened if those now discredited economic systems are the only alternatives to the law of the jungle—a jungle in which they have become the most prosperous and powerful denizens.

In short, they've been able to desensitize their humanity.

I consider myself very fortunate that I could never do that.❖

Fantasy and reality

"What are you reading that junk for?"

The question came from a friend of mine who caught me with *The Path of Daggers*, the latest volume of Robert Jordan's best-selling Wheel of Time fantasy series.

"I read fantasy," I told him, "for the same reason you spend so much time playing golf—to get away for a few hours from the harsh realities of every-day life. We all need some form of temporary escape, and for me it's escape literature—getting lost in an alternative universe. For others it's sports, or hobbies, or TV or movies. And," I added, "really well-written fantasy is not junk."

Like any diversion, of course, all flights from reality can be carried to unhealthy extremes. That happens when people spend too much time evading or denying unpleasant truths, or, even worse, lose the ability to distinguish fact from fiction. Most Canadians, unfortunately, now fall into that category.

The overriding reality in Canada today is that we live in a society ruled by a business and financial élite. Those who fail or refuse to face that reality are living in an unreal world. Not just for a few hours occasionally, as I do when I dip into a fantasy novel, but permanently. And this delusion directs and constrains all their thinking, all their actions and reactions.

To someone who still thinks the country is a democracy with governments that rule in the public interest, the "answer" to social and economic problems is still to be found in politics. Support and elect the "right" party. Lobby the cabinet. Present briefs to parliamentary committees. Stage demonstrations and protests. Make fiery speeches. Fire off angry letters to the editor.

In a democracy, these methods would be appropriate, and often successful. In a plutocracy, however, politicians serve only the rich and powerful, and so actions tailored to a democratic system are futile. Their futility should be obvious, but not to people who mistake the illusion of democracy for the real thing.

Take, for example, the anti-poverty activists. They have been protesting the rise of poverty in Canada for many years. They have lobbied the politicians tirelessly. They have presented reams of briefs and petitions to legislative committees and bureaucrats.

You might think that they would judge the effectiveness of their activities by the results. And if they weren't living in a dream world, they would. They'd see that, despite all their appeals and protests to the politicians, poverty levels were continuing to go up, not down, year after year, and so were the number of food banks. Clearly, the politicians are not concerned about poverty and have no intention of doing anything to alleviate it. Why should they? A plutocracy, by its very nature, is a system that favours the rich and ignores the poor (and those who try to help the poor).

The same aura of unreality affects the great majority of social and community groups, whether they are concerned about health care, child care, unemployment, housing, the environment, pay equity, or any other worthwhile cause. They, too, cling to the mirage of a lost democracy, to the belief that their success can be measured by the number of phone calls they make to their riding MPs.

Admittedly, the illusion of democracy is assiduously maintained by the plutocrats and their political and media minions. It's such a realistic facade that it fools most Canadians. The politicians are adept at playing the role of democrati-

cally-elected representatives of the people, while following
the scripts provided them by the real rulers from their man-
sions and executive suites.

The media reinforce this farce by reporting the politicians'
stage performances as if they were important news rather than
entertainment. As I write this column, the big political story
in Canada is Chrétien's crackdown on the APEC protestors,
and in the United States the ongoing saga of Clinton's carnal
escapades. In Chrétien's case, he was simply following orders from the CEOs who wanted to keep doing business with
Indonesian despot Suharto and didn't want him bothered by
demonstrators. In Clinton's case, he was subservient to the
CEOs, of course, but didn't grovel to them as much as a Republican president would, so his sexual proclivities offered a
means of dragging him down.

In both the Chrétien and Clinton cases, the media frenzy
they unleashed had the added benefit (for the plutocrats) of
distracting people from the really serious economic and social ills troubling their respective countries. In other words,
play up the trivia and play down the crises. Divert and enter-
tain people with the antics of their political leaders, and in so
doing keep the public safely coccooned in a world of fantasy.

The fantasy world is often scary. You could lose your job,
your income, even your home. But it's also, in some sense, a
safe, comfortable and predictable world. One in which you
can always vote in an election, write your MP or MLA, or
take part in a protest march, and hope that eventually these
exercises in democracy will have the desired effect.

To wake up from that dream world, for many people,
would be even scarier because you would then have to face
the grim fact that all the potential solutions to your problems
through the democratic process are no longer available. It's
much easier to reject the reality of corporate rule and keep

acting as if the politicians we elect truly want to serve us rather than their Bay Street masters.

The other deterrent to facing reality is that it raises the thorny question of what, if anything, can be done to over-throw the plutocracy. In a democracy, the electoral system works. So do protests and petitions. And all this make-work activity is ready-made for NGOs and activists. It fills their time. It gives them something to do. It justifies their existence (and sometimes their pay-cheques). But what would be the equivalent measures for challenging corporate rule? Demon-strating in front of the BCNI or Chamber of Commerce of-fices? Sending your briefs and petitions to Tom d'Aquino? Lobbying the CEOs?

Obviously these tactics wouldn't sway the plutocrats, any more than they do the politicians. More direct and pertinent methods would have to be devised. Selective boycotts, per-haps. Shareholder activism. Maybe even the creation of a political party courageous enough to defy the CEOs.

Such strategizing, however, is premature. Who can say at this point how people will want to act if they finally escape from fantasy and come back to the real world? Of course they will want to abandon the no-longer-relevant voting and lob-bying activities that are useless in a plutocracy. But tackling the formidable task of challenging and dethroning our cor-porate rulers will require a lot of thinking, talking and plan-ning. (Tony Clarke has already made a good start in his in-dispensable CCPA book *Silent Coup* and his equally valuable workbook *Challenging Corporate Rule*, which could well be-come the bibles of pro-democracy forces.)

First things first, however, and the first thing is for more Canadians to face up to the reality of corporate rule. An occa-sional excursion into fantasy can be quite therapeutic, but a steady diet of it can be very harmful. For a society no less than an individual.❖

The "good" old days

"The disparity in income between the rich and poor is merely the survival of the fittest. It is merely the working out of a law of nature and a law of God."
— John D. Rockefeller, circa 1894

"We (the transnational corporations) are now in the driver's seat of the global economic engine. We are setting government policies instead of watching from the sidelines."
— David Rockefeller, 1994

In the century between these two pronouncements, the worst excesses of unfettered free enterprise were curbed by regulations and minimum wage standards. Strong unions and progressive governments combined to distribute income more equitably. Social safety nets were fashioned to help those in need.

Corporate owners and executives resisted all these reforms. Their operations had to be forcibly humanized. They always resented having so much of their profits diverted into wages and taxes, but until recently they couldn't prevent it. Now they can.

Thanks to dismantled trade barriers and the new global mobility of capital, they can overcome all political and labour constraints. They are free once more to maximize profits and exploit workers, to control or coerce national governments, to re-establish the law of the jungle as the social norm. We are in danger of reverting to the kind of mass poverty and deprivation that marked the Victorian era.

Unfortunately, most Canadians don't know how badly their forebears were mistreated in the workplaces of the 1800s.

So the prospect of a reversion to Victorian social conditions doesn't alarm them. A brief history lesson may therefore be in order.

Working hours in the mines and factories were from sunrise to sunset, about 72 hours a week. Wages, in 1999 currency, averaged less than $2 a day. Workers had to live in shacks or overcrowded tenements. They couldn't afford carpets on the floor or even dishes for their meals.

Most workplaces were dirty, dimly lit, poorly heated. There were no guards on saw-blades, pulleys or other dangerous machinery, because owners were not held responsible for industrial accidents. Workers took jobs at their own risk. If they were killed or injured while at work, as many thousands were, it was because of their own "carelessness". Uncounted thousands also died from tuberculosis, pneumonia and other diseases caused by inadequate heat or sanitation in their workplaces.

Conditions in the mines were especially bad, with most miners dying from accidents or "black-lung" disease before they reached the age of 30.

Millions of children, some as young as six, were forced to work 12 hours a day, often being whipped or beaten. A Canadian Royal Commission on Child Labour in the late 1800s reported that "the employment of children is extensive and on the increase. Boys under 12 work all night in the glass-works in Montreal. In the coal mines of Nova Scotia, it is common for 10-year-old boys to work a 60-hour week down in the pits.

"These children work as many hours as adults, sometimes more. They have to be in the mill or mine by 6:30 a.m., necessitating their being up at 5 for their morning meal, some having to walk several miles to their work."

This Royal Commission found that not only were children fined for breakages and tardiness, but that in many factories and mines they were beaten with birch rods. Many thousands of them lost their fingers, hands, even entire limbs, when caught in unguarded gears or pulleys. Many hundreds were killed. Their average life expectancy was 33.

As late as 1910 in Canada, more than 300,000 children under 12 were still being subjected to these barbaric working conditions. It wasn't until the 1920s, in fact, that child labour was completely stamped out.

An enterprising union organizer managed to get into a cigar factory in southern Ontario in 1908. He found young girls being whipped if they couldn't keep up their production quota. Many girls wound up at week's end owing the boss money because they had more pay docked for defective cigars than they earned.

A visitor to a twine-making factory in 1907 counted nine girls at one bench alone who had lost either a finger or a thumb. A surgeon who lived in a mill town related in his memoirs that, over a 15-year period, he had amputated over 1,000 fingers of children who had their hands mangled when forced to oil and clean unprotected mill machines while they were still running.

This callous mistreatment of working people was not only condoned, but extolled—and not just by the business establishment. The daily newspapers of the time also defended the employers. So did the major religions. In 1888, when labour leader Daniel O'Donaghue proposed a resolution at a public meeting in Toronto calling for the abolition of child labour, all 41 clergymen who attended the meeting voted against it. In Quebec, for many years, the Catholic Church forbade its members to join a union "under pain of grievous sin"—and many bishops and priests went so far as to deny union members a Christian burial when they died.

Blessed by politicians, the press and the clergy, employers considered it their God-given right to treat workers as virtual slaves.

Said railroad tycoon George F. Baer, "The interests of the labouring man will be cared for, not by the labour agitators, but by the Christian men to whom God has given control of the property rights of the country."

Another robber baron, Frederick Townsend Martin, was even more candid. In an interview he gave to a visiting British journalist, he boasted: "We are the rich. We own this country. And we intend to keep it by throwing all the tremendous weight of our support, our influence, our money, our political connections, our purchased politicians, our public-speaking demagogues, into the fight against any legislation, any political party or platform or campaign that threatens our vested interests."

Today's business executives are not so outspoken, at least not in public, but basically their philosophy today is not much different from that of their 19th-century forerunners. They envy the robber barons of the Victorian era. They want nothing more than to recreate the social and economic conditions that prevailed a hundred years ago.

As David Rockefeller noted, they are back in the driver's seat. They are calling the shots. They have harnessed all governments to their agenda. The only thing they aren't sure about is how long it will take them to obliterate the last vestiges of the welfare state and replace it with their neo-Victorian New World Order.

Already, in most of the developing nations, they have brought back child labour. Conditions in most factories operated by or for the transnational corporations in Asia and Latin America are not much better today than they were in North America and Europe in the 1800s. Hundreds of thousands of boys and girls are being forced to work 12 hours a day in dirty, unsafe workshops, for 40 cents an hour or less.

One 15-year-old girl who started working in a *maquila* sweatshop in Honduras when she was 13 recently testified

before a U.S. Senate subcommittee on child labour. Lesly
Rodriguez told how she and 600 other teenaged girls are
forced to sew cotton sweaters from 6 a.m. to 6 p.m. seven
days a week, forbidden to speak to co-workers, beaten by
their bosses if they make a mistake, allowed only half an hour
for lunch and just two visits a day to the bathroom. She is
paid 38 cents an hour to make sweaters that are sold in the
U.S. under the Liz Claiborne label for $90.

Maybe you think this exploitation of children is possible
only in the Third World—that child labour will never be re-
instated in this country. Think again. As anyone from the
Chamber of Commerce or the Business Council on National
Issues will gladly remind you, the global corporate agenda
calls for Canada to compete with these countries that use child
labour. And the only way to do that, eventually, will be to
put our kids to work, too. The thousands of them already
toiling in the fast-food joints for the bare minimum wage could
well be just the forerunners.❖

PART IV

Corporate Rule: The Effects

Who do we try to rescue today?
Poverty amid plenty
Welcome to the Third World
The downward slide continues
The price of smaller governments
The decline of collectivity

Who do we try to rescue today?

Every day, it seems, there comes another appeal from an organization whose members have been hurt by some kind of government cutback. Whether it's the poor, the sick, the homeless, single mothers, seniors, students, Friends of the Earth, or Friends of the CBC, they all have valid claims on our moral and financial support.

What puzzles me is not that so many groups are being victimized by the corporations' political henchmen. If you're not a member of the business or financial élite or an affluent professional, you're bound sooner or later to be on their hit list. What I find disturbing is that each adversely affected group seems to think that its concerns are the only ones that matter. They don't seem to realize that the attacks on all of them are being engineered by the same sinister masterminds, and that the only chance of stopping them is to pool their resources and launch a concerted counterattack.

The present situation has been likened to a river in which many people—old, young, men, women, white, black, Aboriginal, etc.—are being swept downstream. Strung out along each bank are various rescue teams, one for each sub-category of victims. The seniors' group pulls out the drowning seniors, the anti-poverty group pulls out the poor, the women's group pulls out the women, and so on. It's an evocative metaphor.

Each organization has strong swimmers, and is equipped with ropes and lifebuoys and nets and poles and other rescue equipment. It prides itself on how many people it saves. Not all of them, of course. Many are carried away out of sight and drown. But to rescue even some is considered a great achievement.

These organizations exist to pull people out of the river, or at least make the attempt. That is their *raison d'etre*. Their activities are reactive, not pro-active. This is not to say that their leaders are unaware that somewhere upstream there are other groups, the chuckers or heavers or flingers, whose purpose is to throw people into the river. They know that, and occasionally they will even criticize the chuckers or go and try to reason with them. (They call it "lobbying.")

But that is as far as they will go. They will not seriously try to find out why so many people are being dunked, and who is paying the thugs who do the dunking. If they did, they would find out that there was a privileged minority whose members were never in danger of getting wet—mainly because they were rich and powerful. They were so rich that they could easily afford to pay the heavers and chuckers (sometimes called "politicians") to throw everyone else in the river so they wouldn't have to share any of their booty with them.

It's a pathetic sight when delegates from one of the rescue groups hike up the river to remonstrate with the heavers. "Please stop throwing so many people in the river," they beg. Usually on bended knee.

The thugs promise to stop eventually. Maybe next year. Or the year after that. But they never do. Or they say that they have no choice but to keep filling the river with throwaway people, because there's not enough food or homes or jobs for everyone in a system based on the survival of the fittest. Some have to be discarded, and it's only fitting that they be the weakest and the most helpless.

The rich and ruthless minority will sometimes fool the rescuers by replacing one bunch of chuckers with another. The flingers take over from the heavers, or the slingers take over from the hurlers. "Surely," the rescue organizations reassure themselves, "surely this new gang of people-drowners won't throw in as many as the last bunch." And they don't. They throw in more.

It never seems to occur to the rescue groups to try to find out why all the "politicians" up the river, no matter what they call themselves, continue to keep throwing people in. Or why all the people with the biggest incomes are never among those sacrificed.

Maybe it's because the rescue groups are so busy saving as many victims as they can, so busy collecting donations for their nets and ropes and lifebuoys, that they don't have time to think about changing a system that is so harmful to so many people. Or maybe it's because they are now so accustomed to their role as rescuers, and so organizationally structured, that they can't conceive of a river into which nobody is thrown. How, then, could they justify their existence? On what basis could they continue to appeal for donations?

Now, admittedly, saving people from drowning is a noble pursuit. But preventing them from being tossed in the river in the first place would be even nobler.

Could it be done? We'll never know as long as groups concerned about the drowning of the weak and the poor confine their activities to pulling them out, instead of joining together to confront and foil their political and corporate assailants.

To desist from such a preventive effort is in effect to tolerate a system in which civility and compassion have been displaced by the law of the jungle. It is to concede that there is nothing to be done to change this brutal system except try to rescue and comfort its victims.

Cry me a river.❖

Poverty amid plenty

Eleven years ago, when our honourable Members of Parliament unanimously promised to eradicate child poverty in Canada by the year 2000, they never really intended to do anything of the sort. Or even make the effort.

They were simply doing what politicians habitually do—make promises they know they'll never keep. A book full of such pseudo-promises has even been known to decide the outcome of a federal election.

I used to think that the politicians' indifference to the plight of so many children was because they rarely saw a hungry child. They were aware of the statistical increase in child poverty, but that's all it meant to them: an increase in numbers, not in human misery.

If only, I thought, these million-and-a-half deprived children could be paraded, one by one, down the centre aisle of the House of Commons, so that the MPs could actually see and hear them, surely they would be moved to live up to their promise. Of course, it would take more than a year for all these children to file past our elected representatives; but I thought that even the most unfeeling MP would break down after the first few weeks and decide that these small victims deserved more than a pretension of concern.

Now, of course, I know better. I know that our MPs will never keep their pledge to eliminate child poverty, or even to save many more thousands of children from the same fate. It's not that all politicians are heartless. Many of them no doubt deplore the growing destitution of so many of our youth, and sincerely wish they could do something to help them. But they can't. Their corporate masters—the real rulers of Canada—won't let them.

Consider, if you will, the policies that would have to be undertaken to provide poor children—and necessarily their parents—with a decent standard of living. Unemployment insurance benefits would have to be restored to their 1975 level. Welfare rates would have to be doubled, and so would the minimum wage. Enough additional jobs would have to be created to bring the unemployment rate down to at least 5%. Working mothers would have to be given accessible and affordable child care. Social programs would have to be raised back to their pre-cutbacks standards.

These are all policies to which the CEOs of the largest corporations are adamantly opposed. The bankers, the business executives, the bond-holders and money-lenders—the wealthy and powerful élite who own and run the country—will never permit their political puppets to take such initiatives.

And why not? The answer is simple: for the poor to get more, the rich would have to take less. And the rich have no intention of giving up any part of their disproportionately huge incomes. On the contrary, they intend to keep increasing their share of the national output. Their greed has no limits.

Most of the laws and programs introduced by Canadian governments over the past 20 years have had this underlying purpose: to make the rich and powerful more rich and powerful. The voters, of course, have to be persuaded otherwise, and this has been relatively easy to do. Most people will swallow whatever excuse they're given for government policies that hurt them, whether the excuse is an economic recession, government debt, international competitiveness, or a coffee crop failure in Brazil. The notion that such harmful policies are unnecessary and deliberate would never occur to them.

And so the CEOs, with the help of their minions in the legislatures and their apologists in academe and the media, continue to amass more wealth at the expense of the poor—and increasingly at the expense of the middle class, as well.

The combined wealth of the richest 50 Canadians—all multi-millionaires, of course—now exceeds $40 billion, according to *The Financial Post Magazine*. Assuming that the annual income of the average poor family of four is no more than $25,000, this means that the 50 Canadians at the top of the income ladder have as much money as 1,600,000 low-income Canadian households.

On a global scale, the disparity is much greater. The world's 400 billionaires between them have more money than almost half the world's people: the 2,800,000,000 with the lowest incomes.

To understand the CEOs' unlimited appetite for wealth, you have to be aware that, in an unfettered market-driven society, the wealthier you are, the more power and influence you wield. So a mere million dollars is no longer adequate. Neither is $100 million or even $500 million. Multi-millionaires are now a dime a dozen. To be really powerful these days, you have to become a billionaire. Nothing short of a thousand million dollars will suffice. With that much wealth, you can really be a global mover and shaker.

This is still an exclusive club. So far only eight Canadians or Canadian families have been able to break into it: Kenneth Thomson, the newspaper magnate; the Irving brothers and McCain brothers of New Brunswick; Charles Bronfman of the Seagram Co.; the Eaton family; Ted Rogers of Rogers Communications; W. Galen Weston, the supermarket baron; and Paul Demarais of Power Corp.

The CEOs who have to get by with less than a billion are understandably peeved—and all the more determined to climb into the ranks of the financially exalted. And they now have the means to do so. They have free trade. They have deregulation. They have privatization. They have low or no taxes. They have the freedom to exploit cheap and child labour. They have well-funded think tanks to justify their avarice. They have a mass media propaganda machine to brainwash the population. They have tame politicians to do their bidding.

As the CEOs grab larger and larger shares of the national income pie, more and more Canadians will have to take less, and more and more of us will be forced into pauperism.

That's the stark reality we now face. It is a reality that makes a farce of any political promise to eradicate or even alleviate child poverty in Canada. Keeping that promise would require a more equitable distribution of wealth—something that our corporate rulers will never willingly tolerate.❖

Welcome to the Third World

When Peter Munk, CEO of Horsham Corp., praised former Chilean dictator Augusto Pinochet at one of the company's shareholders' meeting, he was being uncharacteristically candid. Most corporate leaders share his admiration for Pinochet and other despots, but refrain from admitting it in public.

Their affection for tyrants is more than professional courtesy. It's natural that, being autocrats themselves, CEOs would approve of their political counterparts—and envy their ability to crush all opposition. But of course, being concerned mainly with maximizing their profits, their affinity with Pinochet and his ilk is tied directly to the bottom line.

Dictators tend to be very accommodating with transnational corporations (TNCs). They will give them cheap labour, low or no taxes, exemption from minimum employment, health and safety, and environmental standards, and if necessary armed protection from peasant uprisings. All of which translate into massive profits.

As Munk pointed out, Pinochet turned Chile into "the highest profit-per-capita country in the world." It's no coincidence that it also remained a low income-per-capita nation. Under dictatorial regimes, high corporate profits go hand in hand with underpaid and indigent workers.

The TNCs are so delighted with Third World governments which govern solely on their behalf that they want to do away with democracy everywhere. They can't openly install dictators in western countries—at least, not yet—so they have devised an ingenious strategy for replicating Third World conditions—and political systems—in countries they find easy to subvert. Countries like Canada.

All they had to do to suppress democracy here was to gain control of the three major political parties. This was done by infiltrating them, making them dependent on corporate funding, promising their leaders lucrative executive posts when they left politics, or threatening them with an induced economic and financial crisis if they refused to adopt the corporate agenda. With the Tories, Liberals and Reformers all at their mercy, they had the equivalent of a pro-TNC dictatorship, since, no matter what party "won" an election, the only real winners would be Big Business.

Meanwhile, with the help of their media propagandists, they could delude most Canadians into accepting the illusion of democracy as the real thing. Elections would continue to be called and the voters would continue to cast their ballots in the naive hope that changing the governing party would also produce a change of government. Of course, no change is possible when the major parties are controlled by the TNCs. The effect is the same as having a one-party state, the only difference being that most people don't see what a charade their political system has become.

The next step for the CEOs is to convert Canada into a Third World country. They can't do it quickly or overtly, if they want to maintain the semblance of democracy. But the strategy to achieve that goal is well under way.

Third World countries don't have adequate social assistance, so Canadians must be persuaded that their public health care, pension, welfare, and other programs are too generous and too costly, and must be dismantled. Not all at once, but gradually, over several years. The process is accelerating.

Third World countries don't have a well-educated work force. Literacy is not needed for the unskilled service and menial jobs that predominate in a deindustrialized nation. Education and skills training can therefore be confined to the children of the rich who will fill the limited number of professional, technical and managerial positions. Hence the steady and intensifying cuts in public education funding, the encouragement of private schools, and the escalation of university tuition fees.

Third World countries don't have meaningful environmental protection. It's "too costly" for corporations to curb their emissions of toxic waste into the air and water. So regulations aimed at preventing the industrial pollution of the environment must be weakened or withdrawn—or very laxly enforced. Thus we now see the dismantling of Canada's environmental laws and the understaffing of inspection agencies.

Third World countries don't force corporations to pay taxes. Or they tax them very lightly. This policy has already been embraced by most Canadian governments, who are lavish with their corporate subsidies, tax deferrals and exemptions. More than 80,000 profitable companies pay no tax at all, and the corporations' overall share of federal tax revenue, which used to be as high as 20%, is now down to less than 7%—well below the levels in most other countries. The TNCs are still far from happy with their tax "burden" in Canada, but they are confident that they will eventually enjoy a complete and permanent tax holiday.

Third World countries don't have decent wages or effective unions. So real wage levels in Canada must be lowered and the power of unions shackled. This has not been as easy for the TNCs to accomplish as other parts of their agenda, but they have been able to keep workers' real income from rising over the past 20 years. As a result, Canada's average manufacturing wage is now down to 14th on the list of industrialized countries. Keeping two million Canadians out of work and millions of others in part-time or temporary jobs also helps hold wages down and stifle union militancy. Labour law amendments are also being introduced in some provinces that make it more difficult for unions to get certified and to bargain and strike successfully.

Third World countries don't have large or strong public sectors. So it's necessary to privatize Crown corporations and whatever other public services can be taken over and operated at a profit by the private sector. The TNCs would like governments to do nothing more than provide them with the basic services they need—police protection, infrastructure, transportation, and so on—and otherwise let them do whatever they want. Canadian governments are thus slowly being divested of all services that are useful to the people rather than to business.

Third World countries don't regulate or in any way interfere with the operations of the private sector. So, one by one, all such regulations in Canada are being cancelled or so diluted that they have no effect and can safely be ignored. A classic example was Bill C-62, which the Chretien government introduced in 1997. It was designed to allow companies to bypass all health, safety and environmental laws, and instead make separate "compliance" agreements with a cabinet minister. This bill was so outrageous that it failed to get House committee approval and was temporarily withdrawn. But don't be surprised if it's re-introduced and rammed through before the next election. In Third World countries, what business wants, business gets.

In Third World countries a small privileged group at the top owns most of the wealth, while the majority of peo-

ple are mired in poverty. In Canada, this widening of the gap between rich and poor is proceeding on schedule. It still has a long way to go. After all, only about five million Canadians have been driven into poverty so far. That's one of the highest per-capita levels of poverty among the western nations, but still well short of Third World standards. The corporations aren't worried, though. They know all the mechanisms are in place to produce a steady increase in the number of impoverished Canadians. We are bound to sink close to Third World poverty levels before the 21st century is very old.

I could go on with this list indefinitely. **Third World countries don't have a truly democratic government, don't have an independent economy, don't have clean streets, don't have low crime rates.** All of these and other aspects of a truly fair and equitable and prosperous society are also being destroyed in Canada.

The sad irony of this terrible transformation is that most Canadians remain oblivious to it. They have been herded onto the slippery downward slide into Third World wretchedness, but they prefer to believe the United Nations' grotesque ranking of Canada as the best country in the world in which to live, with the United States a close second. "We're No. 1!" they proclaim proudly, as their society crumbles around them.

If they continue to blind themselves to the harsh realities that belie that ludicrously exalted UN status, their gullibility will no doubt reassure their corporate masters.

It gives the TNCs the time and freedom they need to complete their conversion of Canada into a country where Augusto Pinochet would feel right at home. This is not to say that past and present Canadian political leaders such as Brian Mulroney, Jean Chrétien, Paul Martin, Mike Harris and Ralph Klein have not been dutifully subservient to their corporate masters. They certainly have been, and still are. But the TNCs will feel much better when they can dispense entirely with the trappings of democracy and social justice. That may take another 25 or 30 or even 50 years, but they will be content as long as our descent into Third World ranks proceeds unopposed.

Mind you, if enough Canadians became aware of what was being done to their country, they might still be able to stop it. But time is running out, and if they don't soon wake up, it will be too late. Canada will become the first "developed" and democratic country to regress into economic and political serfdom.❖

The downward slide continues

In the preceding essay, *Welcome to the Third World*, first published in the spring of 1997, I accused our corporate rulers of planning to transform Canada into a Third World country.

Neo-liberals scoffed at the idea, of course, and even some activists on the left thought I was being unduly alarmist.

In the intervening period, to hear the right-wingers tell it, Canada has prospered, not declined. Profits have soared, stock markets have boomed, unemployment has fallen to 8%, fewer individuals and companies have gone bankrupt, and governments have cut or eliminated their deficits. Surely the country is on an upswing and not sliding back, as I had predicted.

Well, I'm sorry to sound a discordant note amid all the euphoria, but in fact much of the "progress" recently hailed by CEOs and politicians is more illusory than real. Far too many Canadians remain poor and jobless. Far too many are struggling to cope with stagnant or falling incomes. Far too many are being denied needed health care, education, unemployment insurance, and other social services.

Canada's decline, in short, is proceeding on schedule, even though it is not discernible to most Canadians.

It's not that the commercial media are hiding the evidence of our slow but steady national slump. Not at all. But the newspapers, radio and TV networks are adept at reporting the bad news as apparently isolated and unconnected incidents. Scattered through a newspaper or broadcast, and surrounded by more upbeat news and views, the signs of our decline can easily be mistaken for minor setbacks, not causes for concern.

This is especially true for those Canadians who have trouble making connections—who tend to see the separate strands in a pattern rather than the pattern itself.

An illustration may be helpful. One day last March, I clipped out three articles that appeared in the newspapers and took note of one TV news item the same night. To most readers and listeners, they seemingly had no connection, but in reality they reflected closely linked developments.

The first piece was about a Statistics Canada study of the work force, which found that the three most frequent occupations for men in Canada today are truck drivers, sales clerks, and janitors. For Canadian women, the three most common jobs are sales clerks, secretaries, and cashiers.

The second article reported that the powerful Business Council on National Issues (BCNI), comprised of the CEOs of the top 150 corporations in Canada, had decided that the federal government, despite having eliminated its deficit, should refrain from spending more on social programs, and use its surpluses instead to reduce the federal debt and cut taxes.

The third article described the Chrétien government's refusal to obey a Canadian Human Rights Commission ruling that it grant its female employees pay equity with male employees. The same article reported that a pay equity complaint on behalf of 22,000 Bell Canada workers had been thrown out by Justice Francis Muldoon.

The TV news report was about rising university tuition fees and a survey that found only about one in three young Canadians (36%) are now getting a post-secondary education.

The connection between these four events becomes obvious if you see them all as mileposts on our downward path to Third World status.

The link between the kinds of jobs opening up in Canada and the rising financial barriers to post-secondary education should be crystal clear. As I pointed out three years ago, "Third World countries don't have or need a well-educated work force. A higher education is not required for the unskilled service and menial jobs that predominate in a deindustrialized nation. It can therefore be confined to the children of the rich who will fill the limited number of professional, technical and managerial positions."

The BCNI's call for more social spending cutbacks is also consistent with the drop down to Third World levels. Third World countries don't have universally accessible public health care or pensions or welfare or UI, and so these social programs must be sharply reduced as Canada continues its downward slide.

And so must labour costs. Third World countries don't have fair or decent wages, and they certainly don't have pay equity between male and female workers. Pay equity is thus seen by our corporate overlords as costly and undesirable, and thus something to be fiercely opposed. The objective is to widen this disparity, not narrow it.

The other characteristics of a Third World nation that I cited a year ago are also becoming increasingly more evident. They include the suppression of true democracy, the weakening of environmental safeguards, the failure to make corporations pay their fair share of taxes, the privatization of public agencies and services, the deregulation of corporate activities, the tolerance of ever-widening income disparities, and the sell-off of Canada's economy to foreign corporations and speculators.

And let's not forget the business barons' ongoing propaganda blitz to convince Canadians that all these developments are either beneficial or unavoidable. Millions of Canadians have been led to believe that, but many thousands of others (including you, I hope) have refused to be duped.

The bad news, then, is that our plunge to Third World levels is continuing; and the good news is that, thanks to a growing public awareness, it's not unstoppable.

Not yet.❖

The price of smaller governments

Whenever someone suggests that the federal or provincial governments spend money on something that would benefit most Canadians, not just big business or the financial markets, the kneejerk replies can be anticipated:

"The country can't afford it."

"It would increase government debt."

"The money just isn't there."

Of course, with most Canadian governments now balancing their budgets and many piling up large surpluses, the "we-can't-afford- it" excuse should be wearing pretty thin.

Nobody asked where the money was found for Canada to join in NATO's war in the Balkans, or to hand out billions in subsidies and rarely-repaid "loans" to profitable corporations.

The point is that, whenever the politicians decide to spend money on projects approved by the corporate and financial élite, the money is found. Easily and quickly. It's only when the money is needed for health care or child care or education or for public infrastructure that it becomes scarce.

The Chrétien government proudly tells us that, after its orgy of cutbacks since 1994, it is spending no more now on public services and social programs than was spent in the 1940s—and 30% less than was spent in the "golden age" of the 1960s and early '70s.

That the Liberals feel confident they can make such a boast without offending the electorate underlines the success of the right-wing propaganda attack on "big government." It is now quite politically safe to cut public spending, even when such cuts are as unnecessary as they are economically and socially harmful.

The fact is that public spending has always been a major contributor to Canada's economic growth as well as living standards, providing needed employment in the public sector and also helping to stimulate private sector activity.

In his 1999 CCPA book *Paper Boom*, Jim Stanford refers to the outburst of public spending that occurred during World II, which pulled the country out of a depression, had our factories humming, and created full employment. We could do with another war today, he suggests, to help take up the slack in our current sluggish economy.

Of course he wasn't talking about a shooting war. The kind of "war" he proposed was an all-out effort to rebuild and repair a public sector ravaged by nearly two decades of downsizing and spending cuts.

There's certainly no shortage of worthwhile projects. Stanford's favourite would be the construction of a high-speed rail link between Quebec City and Windsor. As he points out, it would cost about the same, as a share of our GDP (1.2%), as did the construction of the St. Lawrence Seaway back in the 1950s—and would arguably boost our economy as much as the Seaway has.

Nobody opposed the Seaway project, despite its huge cost, and nobody asked, "where's the money coming from?" But the right-wingers are running the show these days, so their claim that we can't afford a super-speed rail service, despite its many positive spinoffs, goes unchallenged.

They are equally effective in blocking all other proposed public spending initiatives, no matter how worthwhile. A super-port in Halifax? Ridiculous! A national child care program? Out of the question! More low-cost housing? Can't afford it! Clean up our polluted air and water? Too costly!

This negative chorus from the right dismisses—even ridicules—all proposed public expenditures that most Canadians would find beneficial. And, since most Canadians have been brainwashed into believing that "the money isn't there any more," they accept the decline of the public sector as unavoidable.

If they sometimes wonder how unlimited government funding somehow magically becomes available for shooting wars, "Team Canada" junkets, corporate tax breaks, and anything favourable to the financial markets and the Business Council on National Issues, they seemingly don't find the contradiction too puzzling.

Stanford also reminds us that there's never a shortage of money to respond to the needs of the victims of natural disasters, such as the people affected by the floods in Manitoba and the ice-storm in Eastern Canada and the Maritimes. These natural disasters, while devastating for the people and communities hit by them, are good for the economy in the sense that the required cleanup and repair work creates jobs and a demand for more private sector goods.

"Why can't we capture these beneficial effects of a disaster," Stanford asks, "without actually having to incur one?"

In other words, why do our governments wait for disasters to force them to open the public purse? Why not launch major pre-emptive campaigns to protect the environment, to repair our potholed highways and dilapidated schools, to provide national child care and pharmacare programs? Such public endeavours would be good investments in a clean environment, in an efficient transportation system, in a safe and prosperous society.

And, right-wing rhetoric notwithstanding, the money for such worthwhile public projects is there—or should be.

The problem is that social spending generates little or no immediate profit for the private sector. In a society driven by corporate and investor greed, that's enough to justify starving the public sector.❖

The decline of collectivity

"I see individual concerns being put ahead of community benefits . . . and I worry about the decline of collectivity in this country. We are becoming increasingly Americanized, which imposes an un-Canadian individualism on our ethic."
—Peter Lougheed
former Tory Premier of Alberta.

"The world's 358 billionaires now have a combined net worth of $760 billion, equal to that of the bottom 45% of the world's population."
—Richard J. Barnet
co-author of "Global Dreams."

These two quotations may seem unconnected, but, as you will soon see, they do go together.

Let's start with Peter Lougheed, whose qualms about "the decline of collectivity" in Canada graced the pages of *Maclean's* magazine.

Never considered a Red Tory—or, in the current hard-right parlance, a "squishy" one—Lougheed was nonetheless alarmed by the extent to which the provincial leaders of his party, notably Ralph Klein and Mike Harris, were pushing the corporate agenda. He was particularly disturbed by their adoption of the American-style cult of individualism, which puts personal rights ahead of community values.

Lougheed didn't go so far as to warn that this trend, if unchecked, would lead to the same social disorder and turmoil that already plagues the United States; but that was the implication of his remarks.

Still, I was surprised that he used the term "collectivity" so appprovingly, as something to be preferred to individualism. Usually conservatives—even "squishy" ones—equate collectivism of any kind with socialism or even communism, and the word leaves their lips dripping with scorn and venom.

They have the advantage of being able to point to both fascist and communist states (Hitler's Germany and Stalin's Russia being the prime examples) where collectivism was taken to the extreme of completely suppressing individual freedom. In the insect world, they can also point to the conformity of the anthill and the beehive.

The consequences of unrestrained individualism, on the other hand, are not so easily demonstrated. Even the social breakdown in the U.S. is not seen by most people as the result of the glorification of individual liberty to the detriment of community (i.e., collective) needs. This is largely because, in a capitalist economic system, any constraint on the freedom of individuals—or, for that matter, individual business firms—is abhorrent, even if such limits are imposed in the broader public interest. To contend, in today's climate of born-again *laissez-faire*, that the common good should be the system's predominant goal is to be guilty of heresy.

Since government was the mechanism devised to protect and advance collective interests, it was inherently hostile to the cult of individualism. So its role had to be reversed. It had to be converted into an instrument for promoting private and individual gains instead. Its purpose henceforth was to break the "legislative shackles" that had been clamped on individual freedom.

Regulations that had curbed the socially harmful activities of individual persons and companies were weakened or eliminated. Social programs that helped the poor and unemployed, and thus interfered with the workings of the market system, were gutted. Public institutions and services that allegedly could be provided more efficiently by entrepreneurs were privatized. Taxes that "stifled or crippled" private initiative were cut.

"The best government," we were told by its wreckers, "is the least government."

Governments have thus been transformed from guardians of the public interest to boosters of private profit, from promoters of social justice to destroyers of the welfare state. It matters not at all, apparently, that the only beneficiaries of this anti-government rampage are the big corporations and the wealthy élite. The other 90% of us should be content that we are now as free as the plutocrats to dine at the Ritz, shop at Harrod's, and spend our winters on the Riviera. And they, for their part, are as free as we are to dine at McDonald's, shop at Zeller's, and spend their winters shovelling snow.

The champions of individual rights now reign supreme. But their triumph, if prolonged, will exact an intolerably high price—not just from the jobless and the dispossessed, but from the economy, and indeed from the entire human species. Why? Because it rests on a philosophy that is fundamentally foolish and dangerous.

This is the peculiar notion that, if each person and corporation is left free to pursue individual advantage, the "market" will make sure that the overall result will benefit society as a whole. In fact, the outcome is the precise opposite. The strongest, the luckiest, the most ruthless prosper, but the rest—deprived of collectivist safeguards—are victimized.

It is one of the worst flaws of human nature that the actions we take as individuals may benefit us separately, at least in the short term, but hurt us collectively. These individual actions can be reasonable, even brilliant, if assessed purely on the basis of their immediate personal gains; but collectively they can prove disastrous.

The invention of the combustion engine was a giant forward step in human mobility. Each person driving a car benefits individually, but millions doing the same thing poison the air we all have to breathe.

One person carrying a handgun for protection may be acting intelligently as an individual. Millions doing the same thing create a violent and dangerous society.

A company that automates and computerizes its operations benefits from laying off half its employees; but when all businesses do the same thing, the ensuing collapse of consumer spending reduces their sales and profits and leads to a recession.

A business genius, free to amass unlimited wealth, enjoys an opulent lifestyle, but the billions of dollars he hoards are unavailable to help the 12 million children who die every year from hunger or disease—deaths preventable for a few pennies each. (As noted above, $760 billion in the hands of just 358 people is surely the ultimate in senseless and obscene individualism.)

The basic point, I suppose, is that unrestrained individualism can be even worse for a society than unrestrained collectivism. Curtailing and humanizing individual enterprise doesn't mean we have to become like the ants or the bees; but it does mean that some limits, some regulations, some minimum standards have to be in place to protect collective rights and meet collective needs.

Otherwise we degenerate into a neo-Victorian society scarred by huge income disparities, masses of poor and jobless, urban slums, and high levels of crime and social unrest.

That process of social decay is already well under way in Canada, and it will continue as long as our governments remain devotees of the cult of individualism.❖

PART V

Corporate Rule: The Servants

A lament for democracy
Tips on what (not) to read
Let's ignore the politicians
Let's outlaw broken promises
The corporate devolution script
Alternative budget policies—and packaging
"Good corporate citizenship"

A lament for democracy

"You can always get the truth from a politician—after he retires."
—Wendell Phillips.

"Nothing is politically right which is morally wrong."
—Daniel O'Connell.

My manifestly low opinion of the current crop of politicians has led some of my faithful readers to infer that I am anti-government.

Of course I'm not. I agree with Edmund Burke's description of government as "a human contrivance to provide for human needs." He was referring, however, to all human needs—not the needs of a small privileged élite.

It's the politicians today who have given government a bad name. They are the ones who are openly and blatantly anti-government. Instead of governing in the interests of all citizens, they are operating a catering service for the rich and powerful. And when you reduce government to that limited function, you can safely dismantle the four-fifths of government that would otherwise serve the majority of people.

The Chrétien Liberals, for example, are now boasting that they have shrunk the size of the federal government—in terms of its spending as a percentage of GDP—to the size it was back in 1949, well before most of our social programs were established.

The rich and powerful don't need public health care or public education or public pensions or unemployment insurance or any of the other programs and services that they can easily afford to provide for themselves. What they resent is having to help pay for these services for their less-well-off fellow citizens.

In the past, when politicians felt morally obliged to govern on behalf of everyone, they did their best to maintain universal services, and kept unemployment and poverty as low as they could. Now that they serve only bankers, business executives and investors, they can confine government activities to those that are needed or approved by the corporate hierarchy: basic infrastructure, communications, transportation, police protection, international relations, along with monetary and fiscal policies that favour lenders over borrowers, business over labour, sellers over buyers, polluters over environmentalists.

There was a time when most politicians could not be bought, bribed, or intimidated. Now, all but a few of them— some reluctantly, most willingly—have been corrupted. They have become servants of the corporate overlords. The corporations are the source of their campaign funds, their legislative agenda, their media and academic apologists, their lucrative consulting and directorial posts when they leave politics.

To get elected, of course, the politicians have to pretend to be concerned about the other 90% of the population. They have to convince the voters that, even when they chop services and facilitate more layoffs, even when they further widen the gap between rich and poor, they are somehow still trying to help all of us.

You might think this would be a hard sell, but in fact it has been remarkably easy to persuade voters to elect governments who will spend the next four or five years pummeling them. The more they are hurt or abused, the more likely they are to re-elect their political assailants. Ralph Klein is a good example, and Mike Harris was also rewarded with a second term by his victims.

The power of the corporate propaganda machine is truly awesome. The CEOs of the biggest transnationals own or control the media, and when they use their media to spread lies, the lies become the conventional wisdom—or the "common sense." Recall how they trumpeted the alleged benefits of free trade during the 1988 election. Free trade, they and their political mouthpieces earnestly assured us, would create more jobs, and wouldn't harm our social programs. These lies deceived enough voters to give the Mulroney government a second chance to put the boots to us—and we're still licking our wounds.

Of course it doesn't really matter any more which political party forms a government. The Liberals are as slavishly devoted to their corporate masters as the Tories are. So is the Reform party. NDP politicians may not be such dutiful servants of big business, but basically they do as they're told by Bay Street, too, if not as speedily or with the same ideological zeal. They haven't been bought or bribed, but they have been intimidated. They also feel—to be fair to them—that they have to follow the bulk of the brainwashed electorate into the right of the political spectrum, where the right-wing propaganda machine has dragged them.

What are the prospects of ever again getting a government that would truly govern on behalf of all Canadians? Of ever again getting politicians we can trust and respect?

It won't happen as long as we keep losing the propaganda war. As long as most people are deluded into believing that free market forces must prevail, that the best government is the least government, that we are helpless pawns in the game of global competition, then we will continue to get the kind of disastrous governance that now prevails—no matter which bunch of corporate flunkeys we choose to favour with our ballots.

To get serious about fighting the propaganda war, we have to create our own left-of-centre-oriented media. It's not enough to develop strong critiques and workable alternatives

to the corporate agenda if our message is not seen or heard
except by the already converted minority who read *The Canadian Forum, The CCPA Monitor, Canadian Dimension, This
Magazine, Briarpatch,* and other out-of-the-mainstream publications.

Right now, we're in a war in which we have lots of good
ammunition, but only slingshots to deliver it. So we are reduced to asking our enemies to let us borrow their guns to
shoot our shells back at them. Little wonder we are not scor-
ing many hits. We should have learned by now that any hope
of restoring true democracy in Canada, and with it a better
breed of politicians, depends largely on creating a better informed electorate.❖

Tips on what (not) to read

"So many books . . . So little time . . ."

That's the rueful sentiment displayed on one of my favourite sweatshirts. It pithily reflects the frustration of avid
readers faced with more reading material than they can possibly peruse.

The only solution is to be scrupulously selective. Don't
read anything that confuses fact with fiction, such as most of
the mainstream media. Eschew the rantings of tiresome right-
wing ideologues like Andrew Coyne, Barbara Amiel, Terence
Corcoran and Diane Francis.

One of the best ways to create time for really useful books
and magazines is to refrain from reading, watching or listen-
ing to anything about politics and politicians. Given the enormous space and time in the media devoted to their legislative posturing, this frees up an amazing number of hours that
would otherwise be lost.

Many people still believe we have a democracy in Canada,
and that we should therefore follow closely the activities of

our governments. After all, they argue, the policies the politicians favour and the laws and regulations they enact can affect our lives and livelihood, sometimes quite significantly. True enough. But, because these policies and laws are now drafted in the Bay Street boardrooms and the offices of the Business Council on National Issues, their enactment in the legislatures has become a mere formality. An anti-climax. Like Lola, what the corporations want these days, the corporations get. Their political lackeys see to that. And what the corporations want is rarely of any benefit to the rest of us.

They wanted free trade; we didn't; so we got free trade. They wanted the GST; we didn't; so we got the GST. They wanted massive cuts in Medicare, education and unemployment insurance; we didn't; so we got the cuts. They wanted deregulation and weaker safety and environmental laws; we didn't; so we got more dangerous workplaces and a polluted environment. They wanted a tax system that takes little from them and lots from us; we didn't; so we got an unfair tax system. The list goes on and on. Why continue to expect anything different in the future, as long as big business controls our governments and sets their priorities?

To keep taking the politicians seriously, to treat them as anything but business flunkeys, serves only to sustain the illusion that it is they, not their corporate masters, who are responsible for all the economic and social ills being inflicted on us.

Granted, there is some entertainment value in the antics of the people we elect to neglect our needs and pass our tax payments on to the bankers and CEOs. Their pretension that it is the voters they serve, not their corporate masters, has its laughable aspects. Their bombast and blustering can be amusing. So can their elaborate attempts to disguise their servile adherence to the corporate agenda.

As long as you know that the legislative debates, the committee hearings, the election promises, and all other political activities are now theatrical events, divorced from reality, no harm (other than wasting time) is done by reading about them or watching them on television.

Personally, however, if I'm in the mood to be entertained by the hired help, I prefer to watch reruns of "Upstairs, Downstairs." At least, the household staff in that superb BBC TV series didn't pretend to be anything more than servants. Our politicians, however, despite having agreed always to do the bidding of the business barons, continue to act as if they were still running the country. And to make it even worse, they're terrible actors.

To really find out how the country is being ruled, and what our rulers have in store for us, all you have to do is read the *Financial Post* and the *Report on Business* section of the *Globe and Mail*. This is where the big corporations tell us what their priorities are and what they expect from their political minions on Parliament Hill and in the provincial legislatures.

None of the concessions to the corporations came as a surprise to me. I knew free trade was coming, I knew the GST was coming, I knew our social programs would be gutted, I knew about all the tax breaks and handouts to the corporations—long before they became legislative realities. I didn't have to read the political "news" or listen to the parliamentary "debates," because these were all demands the tycoons had previously aired publicly in the *Globe and Mail* and the *Financial Post*. The only thing in doubt was exactly when the politicians were going to give their masters what they wanted. Usually it was as soon as they could cook up some excuse to feed to the gullible citizens who would be hurt by all these boons to business.

The current outcry from the CEOs is for even lower business and "payroll taxes," which is what they call their minimal share of the cost of UI, public pensions, and workers' compensation. Never mind that these modest contributions from employers are already lower in Canada than they are in most other Western countries. "We want them down even lower," the CEOs insist, and their legislative toadies will no doubt soon comply.

(I'm reminded of H.L. Mencken's gibe that you can always tell a politician by his or her breath, because it reeks of the finest shoe-polish.)

Getting back to ways of making more time for worthwhile reading, it follows that, just as you save time by spurning media coverage of what now masquerades as parliamentary democracy in Canada, you gain even more time by disengaging from all other political activities. Don't bother to write or phone or lobby your MPs or MLAs, or waste time preparing briefs to submit to them. It will be futile. So will demonstrations and protests. These would only have a chance of working if we lived in a real democracy. In a system where politicians get their votes from us but take their marching orders from big business, all you accomplish by lobbying and demonstrating is to prop up the facade of democracy and perpetuate corporate rule.

If you really do have an irresistible urge to complain about the dismantling and "Third Worldizing" of Canada, at least confront the people who are actually responsible—the CEOs of the big transnational corporations, the financiers and money-lenders. They have offices in most Canadian cities. Do your lobbying and demonstrating there. Mind you, it won't have any more effect than pleading with the politicians, but at least you'll be targeting the real perpetrators of our decline as a nation.

Your time will be much better spent, however, reading about political, social and economic realities. There are magazines and books that tell you what is really happening. *The*

CCPA Monitor. THIS Magazine and *Canadian Dimension.*
Briarpatch. Linda McQuaig's *The Cult of Impotence.* Murray
Dobbin's *The Myth of the Good Corporate Citizen.* Michael
Moore's *Downsize This!* Marci MacDonald's *Yankee Doodle
Dandy.*

I'm not advocating a policy of pacifism or appeasement
or non-involvement. What I'm proposing is that Canadians
stop wasting their time reading about and watching political
soap operas, and concentrate instead on learning how their
country was taken over by the TNCs.

Only when enough of us reach that level of comprehen-
sion will we be able to think realistically about how to over-
throw our corporate rulers and restore true democracy in
Canada. And get mad enough to make the effort.❖

Let's ignore the politicians

When you come to understand that it is the corporations—
along with the other members of the upper class—who now
control our political system and set its agenda, you come to
see that the politicians we elect have no real power. They often act as if they do, but that's all it is—an act. The butler, as it
were, pretending to be the lord of the manor.

As the corporations' lackeys, the politicians dutifully pass
laws and adopt policies that favour business and the rich.
They meekly carry out their orders to slash social programs,
gut Medicare, underfund education, throw people off UI and
welfare, and shift more of the tax load from the rich to the
middle class.

As a reward for doing their business bosses' dirty work,
government leaders—the most prominent cabinet ministers—
are given lucrative executive posts on Bay Street or on company boards when the voters finally get fed up and throw
them out of office. The same reward awaits their replacements

from another party, who can be counted on to be just as servile to the country's corporate rulers.

The illusion of democracy, however, continues to be maintained. The media keep telling us what our politicians are doing and saying, as if that really matters any more. And even worse, the people and organizations who are being hurt the most by what governments are doing to them are still reacting as if these harsh laws and policies originate with the politicians—as if they were not being dictated by the big corporations, by the wealthy, by the banks, the bond-holders, and by the International Monetary Fund.

I think that the leaders of most unions, churches, community groups and social coalitions now realize that we no longer have a democratic form of government in Canada—that we live under a system of corporate rule. But unfortunately they still behave as if it is the politicians who are governing the country—politicians who remain susceptible to protests and appeals.

So they stage demonstrations outside the legislatures. They write or phone or visit their MPs or MLAs. They write briefs to be presented to parliamentary committees. When they are asked by the media to respond to a government action they oppose, they lash out at the government or at the minister involved, instead of putting the blame where it belongs: on the masters rather than the servants.

It's true the politicians must share the blame for the dismantling of our welfare state. The excuse that they were only following orders is no more valid for them than it was for Adolph Eichmann. Most of them, in fact, are wielding the axe against our basic institutions, programs and values with a zest and brutality that draws the effusive praise of their corporate masters.

However, to direct all our anger and opposition against the minions—to devote all our efforts to changing their minds—is to reinforce the mistaken notion that it is they who are calling the shots. We thereby help prop up the facade that now passes for democracy in Canada. And we let our real tormentors hide behind that facade and enjoy the anonymity of their executive suites.

When will left-wing political activists stop acting as if we still lived in a democracy and turn their protests against the business barons, bankers, and billionaires? When will they start staging their protests in front of the Bay Street business towers? When will they start targeting business leaders instead of the business leaders' political lackeys? When will they start to tap the vast potential of union pension funds to challenge corporate power? When will they start to mobilize their collective strength as consumers to boycott the most offensive corporations?

The activists seem to have three excuses for carrying on with the present charade. The first is simply inertia. They've always objected to laws and government actions they dislike by going after the politicians, and so they have trouble redirecting their attacks.

The second reason is that they believe that many of the backbenchers are unhappy with their government's decisions and can be prodded into resisting them. This is wishful thinking at best. Some backbenchers may indeed be uncomfortable with the cabinet's policies, but, apart from the rare Warren Allmand, they won't dare defy them. Not if they want to retain any hope of joining the inner circle themselves, or getting plum committee posts and overseas junkets.

The third reason is the most ostensibly persuasive, in that the protesters can point to a few apparent successes from their appeals to the politicians. Some of the most severe proposed cutbacks are reduced, some of the more draconian clauses in a bill moderated. "See!" the lobbyists crow. "We forced them to back down!"

In fact, the legislation is deliberately worded in extreme terms and the desired cuts inflated so that the government can make these "concessions" and then claim that they "listened to the people." The end result of this cynical ploy is that the protesters are appeased and the political system portrayed as democratic, when in fact the government ultimately makes exactly the cuts and laws that its business masters demand.

It's time this farce was recognized for what it is. It's time for the victims of corporate rule to stop trying to influence the corporations' political henchmen and turn their protests against those who now brandish all the real power—the country's corporate and financial élite.

And who are they? They're on the list of the most highly-paid business executives. They're the members of the Business Council on National Issues, the Boards of Trade, the Chambers of Commerce. The Top 50 of them—the richest among us—were listed in the *Financial Post* magazine, starting with Kenneth Thomson, the newspaper magnate who owns the *Globe and Mail* and is worth $8.2 billion, and going down to No. 50 on the list, Charles Rathgeb, a former construction company executive who is forced to scrape by with a mere $145 million.

In the title of his last book, Dalton Camp asked, "Whose country is this, anyway?"

It's theirs. And they'll keep it as long as their victims, the vast majority of Canadians, remain unaware that they now live under corporate rule.❖◆

Let's outlaw broken promises

When I originally wrote this piece, in early summer 1998, the papers were full of stories about government patronage, secrecy, lies and broken promises. From supplying India, Pakistan, China and Turkey with nuclear weapon technology to lavishing untendered contracts on Bombardier, from cheating the unemployed of UI benefits to breaking a promise to rescind the GST on books, from backing down on pledges to reduce poverty to reneging on greenhouse gas emission targets—the sorry tale of politics in Canada today played itself out.

None of these stories deserved media coverage, any more than would reports that grass grows, the sun shines, or rain falls. Under our political system, this is how politicians behave. This is their normal, everyday routine. This is what they do for a living. They lie, mislead, misrepresent, falsify and fabricate. They engage in all kinds of knavery because the system not only tolerates it, but rewards it.

Not only that, but most people know that politicians are scoundrels. Nine out of 10 Canadians in a recent poll said they believed politicians lie to get elected, and a smaller majority thought that "quite a few politicians" in a government party are crooks. So why is it considered newsworthy when politicians act like politicians? How else would they act, and what else is there for them to do in a system in which they are only the make-believe rulers?

The real rulers—the corporate CEOs and financiers—don't much care about the shenanigans in the Parliament Hill servants' quarters as long as the servants do what they're told. And if the servants occasionally moonlight as burglars or con artists or stand-up comics, and if these antics preoccupy the press and the public, well, that's the circus part of the bread and circuses.

Some thoughtful and otherwise intelligent Canadians do let themselves be diverted by the politicians and their seemingly inexhaustible forms of skullduggery. They fret about voter cynicism, about the erosion of real democracy, about the politicians' total disregard of the people who elect them.

The political pundits have come up with several ideas for making the politicians accountable. Most of these ideas involve some proposal to keep cabinet ministers from ignoring the electorate between elections. Various kinds of proportional representation have been suggested. So has the holding of referenda on crucial issues. A few legislatures have already instituted "recall" provisions for the most egregious misconduct, though none of them has yet proved workable.

There are two big shortcomings with all these ideas. The first is by far the worst, even though it seems to be obvious only to a few people besides me. That is the subservience of all political parties (most willingly) to the corporate overlords. In this reality, it doesn't much matter what gang of politicians gets to form the government. They're all going to follow the corporate agenda, anyway. And that won't change by converting to a rep-by-pop system, or setting up constituent assembles, or replacing the most nefarious politicians in mid-term. Even referenda would turn out to be ineffectual on most issues, since the corporate-controlled media can usually sway public opinion in the corporations' favour.

The second problem with the "reforms" proposed so far is that they really wouldn't do much to make the politicians accountable, even if corporate rule were overthrown and some politicians really were willing and able, hypothetically, to govern in the public interest. Parliamentary "democracy" can never be truly democratic as long as politicians can make promises to the voters that they are free to break with impunity for the next four or five years. Any system in which the voters can never be sure they'll get what they voted for—and could even get the exact opposite—can't be described as even nominally democratic.

Given the reality of corporate rule, it's daydreaming even to speculate on what reforms would be needed to make the parliamentary system truly work for the Canadian people.

But, what the heck, let's daydream a bit and pretend that corporate rule has collapsed and that there's broad public support for needed reforms to make politicians honest and the system itself responsive to public needs and concerns.

The first task would be to prohibit political perfidy. This would mean that promises made during election campaigns would have to be kept, so that voters would have some real— and reliable—alternatives to pick from. A useful model—useful even considering its source—could be the U.S. Republican party's "contract with America," except that in Canada a party's list of election promises would be a binding contract with the voters. It would have the same effect as a legal document, with severe penalties for violations: not just impeachment, but heavy fines and even jail terms for the most blatant treachery. (Refusing to fulfill the promise to scrap the GST, for example, would have netted all members of the Chrétien cabinet six months in the slammer.) If backbenchers were also held accountable for government backsliding, not just cabinet members, it would give them an incentive to be more than trained seals and rubberstampers.

Under such enforced accountability, parties would be more likely to tell voters what they would *really* do if they formed a government. And their promises would have to be clearly and precisely worded, so that they couldn't claim later that the voters had misunderstood them. A party would have the option, of course, of not making any promises at all, but in that case would be unlikely to garner much support.

There are two arguments against binding a government to promises it makes during an election, and these would have to be addressed. The first is that the new government hadn't realized how badly the previous regime had mishandled the finances, and now found, regrettably, that the resources just weren't there to keep promises that involved extra government spending. To preclude that excuse, the outgoing government would be compelled to open its books and accounts to the opposition parties, so there would be no post-election surprises.

The second argument is that it's impossible to anticipate what will happen during the four or five years of a government's mandate. The economy could take a nosedive, the dollar could collapse, inflation could take off, B.C. could vote to secede, Upper Volta could declare war on us. A government has to have the flexibility to respond to these unexpected events, even if it means breaking election promises.

Okay, true enough. But the unpredictability of the future is not a valid reason to take the politicians off the hook. It can be built into the election "contract" in two ways. The first is to incorporate into their list of promises the aspiring parties' planned reaction to unforeseen events. What would they do if the economy flagged or heated up? How would they address a rekindling of inflationary pressures? What's their policy on a B.C. breakaway?

Given that not all social, economic, and constitutional developments can be foreseen and adequately prepared for, the keeping of election promises would also be referred to an impartial tribunal. Such a tribunal—the composition of which I leave to others to determine—would be charged with overseeing the adherence to promises, and to hearing arguments for and against their violation. It would also be invested with the judicial authority to impose penalties on politicians found guilty of breaking promises without valid reason.

Of course I'm fantasizing. The introduction of such an accountability mechanism would require radical constitutional and legislative amendments. It would involve a major restructuring of the whole system of parliamentary democracy. All the experts will say that such a fundamental change in the political status quo can't or shouldn't be made, or even contemplated.

Okay. But in that case let's stop pretending that the status quo delivers more than a semblance of democracy, or that it could be made genuinely democratic with just some minor tinkering. That point of view reflects a flair for fantasy even greater than mine.❖

The corporate devolution script

Canadians concerned about the dismantling of federalism and the devolution of Ottawa's rights and duties to the provinces may not be aware that this is an integral part of the corporate agenda.

The fact is, however, that the provincial premiers, in demanding—and getting—more and greater jurisdictional powers, are closely following a blueprint mapped out for them by the country's corporate élite.

Pulling the strings of its political puppets behind the scenes is the powerful Business Council on National Issues (BCNI), the cabal of CEOs who run the 150 largest companies in Canada.

The BCNI is not trying to hide its plans for a disunited federation. On the contrary, it spelled them out in great detail about three years ago at a conference it hosted in Ottawa—a conference it called, with a straight face, "Building a Stronger Canada."

According to the BCNI, this could best be done by shrinking and weakening the national government, and turning over most of its rights and responsibilities to the provinces. All that would be left in the federal jurisdiction, basically, would be national defence, international trade, and monetary policy.

In its *Agenda for Action*, adopted at the close of the conference, the BCNI called on the federal government to abandon all responsibility for mining, forestry, housing, tourism, regional development, municipal affairs, recreation and sports. It would also be expected to turn over to the provinces most of its responsibilities for fisheries, agriculture, the environment, culture, communications, and industrial development, and to "retreat" from labour market training, social housing, child care, and student loans.

At this conference—attended, incidentally, by many top-level provincial officials—the BCNI deplored the federal government's role as a setter and enforcer of national standards. "The social and economic union," its *Agenda for Action* declared, "has not been well-served by the unilateral imposition of federal standards and rules." Better by far, the CEOs assured us, to have a "leaner" and non-interventionist federal government, so that the provinces could each be free to set its own standards for health care, education, social security, and other basic services.

The BCNI's prescription for "saving" Canada, in short, was to dismember it. In such a patchwork federal system, individual Canadians would receive widely disparate levels of service, depending on the province in which they happened to live.

As former Manitoba Premier Howard Pawley remarked at the time, "Had such a restriction of the federal power been in effect 30 years ago, it would have prevented the establishment of Canada's present health care system. Any chance of a future government introducing a national child care program will be eliminated."

This was the same disunity agenda the CEOs tried to implement earlier through the Charlottetown Accord. Fortunately, they miscalculated by allowing it to be put to a referendum, giving Canadians a chance to reject it. Now the strategy is to achieve the same objective, incrementally, undemocratically, in closed-door sessions between the provincial premiers and Ottawa.

Anyone who doubts that the premiers—all of them, without exception—are dutifully following the BCNI's decentralization script should have a look at the "final communiques" that have been issued by the Annual Premiers' Conferences in recent years.

The communique emanating from the 1995 conference stated that the provinces "must take on a leadership role with respect to...areas of provincial jurisdiction and speak with a common voice in the debate on social policy reform."

By the time of the 1997 conference, this position had hardened into a strong statement that "federal unilateralism must end."

Cindy Wiggins of the Canadian Labour Congress says it is clear from the conference communiques and background papers that the main objective of the premiers is to further reduce overall spending on social programs.

"Their rationale is pessimistic, regressive, and narrowly focused on fiscal concerns rather than on the public interest," she said. Clearly, the premiers have bought into the BCNI vision of a future low-wage, high-unemployment nation that can no longer afford such "excessively costly" levels of health care, education, UI, welfare, pensions, and other government-provided services.

In one communique, the premiers stress the need for social programs to be "responsive to changing social and economic conditions [and] regional priorities," which is another way of saying they should vary from province to province.

Wiggins concludes, after carefully studying all the communiques, that the premiers' blueprint "involves a massive stripping of federal power in the provision of key social programs." The federal government would no longer have any right to enforce national standards, but instead would be "reduced to one of 13 'partners' around the federal-provincial-territorial negotiating table."

Since the BCNI also dictates policy at the federal level, it comes as no surprise that the Chrétien government is complicit in its own enfeeblement. Its willingness to accommodate the BCNI's disunity goal was reflected in its 1996 Speech from the Throne, in which it pledged that it "will not use its spending power to create new cost-shared programs in areas of provincial jurisdiction without the consent of the majority of the provinces."

This statement, along with other federal concessions to the provinces, amounts to an abandonment of Ottawa's historic constitutional rights and obligations. Arguably its most important responsibility has been to ensure that all Canadians have equivalent access to public programs and services. This was a fundamental principle of the federation, and it served us well in building a more caring and more equitable society than would otherwise have been possible.

The big corporations, however, always disapproved of such a society in Canada, because it curtailed their own power. People with jobs and social security are more difficult to control and manipulate. So they have to be made more insecure and desperate, and thus more subservient to corporate rule.

The decentralization of Canada is key to the BCNI's divide-and-conquer strategy. It will be much easier for the corporations that make up the BCNI to exploit our resources and our people if the power of the federal government to protect the public interest is dissipated among the provinces.

The people of Canada were able to block the BCNI's previous disunification effort by voting it down in the Charlottetown Accord referendum. The challenge now facing Canadians is to find some equally effective way of foiling this latest BCNI plot.❖

Alternative budget policies— and packaging

When the CCPA and CHO!CES release their annual alternative federal budget (AFB), usually in early February, it is given scant coverage by the commercial press. A few paragraphs on an inside page, if that. The broadcast media, especially the CBC, tend to be more receptive, mentioning the AFB in newscasts, interviewing some of our main budget-drafters, and even reporting the AFB highlights without too much distortion.

On the CBC National Magazine, CCPA and CAW economist Jim Stanford debated the merits of the AFB with the chief economist of the Royal Bank, John McCallum. McCallum's chief criticism of the AFB was that, in preparing it, our economists had "totally ignored the market reaction, which would be visceral, and will give you much higher interest rates." If the AFB were implemented, he warned, "the markets would go berserk."

"Why do the markets behave that way, then?" Stanford asked him. "Is it because they don't like health care and they don't like social investment?"

"Markets sometimes do crazy things," McCallum admitted. "But we don't control those markets, so it's best to stay on the good side of them."

In other words, he was saying that no federal budget will work unless it has the blessing of the country's powerful financial interests. Our big mistake, in putting together an alternative budget that would benefit the vast majority of Canadians, was that we hadn't first run it past the Bay Street boys.

You can be sure Paul Martin would never make that mistake.

The reaction of most business leaders and right-wing pundits to the AFB was predictably to ignore it. If it did get mentioned at all by editorial writers and columnists, it was to ridicule it as an irresponsible call to return to the overspending, deficit-burdening ways of the past.

One of the few columnists who agree with the AFB's approach and purpose, Susan Riley of *The Ottawa Citizen*, chided us for the dullness and unoriginality of our document. It needed clever graphics, colour charts, and one or two (not a hundred) compelling ideas, she argued. She thinks the left as a whole needs more colour and pizzazz, more novelty and imagination, "something amusing, memorable and incisive," and a charismatic leader—"a latter-day Oscar Wilde—to deliver the script."

She has a point. Many of us on the left tend to be all too earnestly censorious and sometimes tediously righteous. We're prone to lecture rather than inspire, and our prose doesn't often sparkle with metaphor and wit. On the other hand, we do have our share of bright and articulate writers and speakers. Like the aforementioned Jim Stanford. Like Linda McQuaig and Maude Barlow. Like Tony Clarke and Jim Laxer. Like Susan Riley's fellow Southam columnist Charles Gordon and *The Toronto Star*'s Tom Walkom.

The flaw in Riley's criticism is that having the snazziest publications and the wittiest speakers would not guarantee us equal space and time in the media with the free-market ideologues. We will always be limited to a fraction of their space and time in trying to deliver our alternative policies to the masses. I would even predict that, the more colourful and inspirational our messages (and messengers) became, the more our share of the commercial media would shrink. We'd probably be cut from our present 3% to maybe 1%.

I must confess that I've always been skeptical of the alleged need to convey our thinking in more colourful packages. Would the CCPA's magazine *The Monitor*, for instance, be more attractive and readable if we dressed it up with cartoons and photos and fancy designs? We could add those accessories without much extra expense, I suppose, but would they really enhance readability? I happen to think (and I readily confess this bias as editor) that what makes any publication readable is the quality and clarity of the text and headlines. As long as there's some variety in the length and tone of the articles, some leavening of the deadly serious ones with dollops of satire and humour, then the overall effect in my view is satisfying. Maybe even aesthetic.

What *The Monitor* seeks to do is to give its readers in every issue at least a few new bits of knowledge, a few new insights, that will enlarge their world-view and stimulate their intellects. To clutter up the pages with graphics would mean displacing two or three such articles—and for some readers the pieces discarded could be the ones they would have found most enlightening.

But I digress. What Susan Riley was concerned about is something that concerns many of us on the left, which is how best to demolish the myths that underpin the New World Order, and to persuade more people that there are better and viable alternatives to the corporate agenda.

I used to think that was a goal that couldn't be achieved without having our own media outlets, and I still favour such an undertaking, but lately I've become more optimistic. The failures and destructive effects of free-market capitalism have become so pronounced that it has been widely discredited, its malignance and long-term unworkability on display for all to see. Its most strident proponents have become, in effect, our involuntary allies.

Even some of the one-time ardent advocates of the New World Order—people like World Bank economist Joseph Stiglitz and financier George Soros—are now openly calling for regulatory reforms and a more equitable distribution of wealth and power. They're still very much in the minority among the business and financial élites, but their voices are louder (and arguably more influential) than ours.

It's far too soon to anticipate that globalization will self-destruct, or be brought down by its critics from within and without. But the free-market edifice is definitely showing cracks that the champions of goodness and fairness (not to put too fine a point on it, us) may be able to take advantage of in the years ahead.❖

"Good corporate citizenship"

The title of this piece is an oxymoron, as author Murray Dobbin quite effectively demonstrated in his book *The Myth of the Good Corporate Citizen*. Most corporations today feel no responsibility to the communities or countries where they may happen (for the time being) to be located. Indeed, most of them now admit that for them national boundaries don't exist any more. They say they can't afford to favour any country or region, other than those that offer them the lowest wages and taxes, and the weakest environmental laws.

The commercial media owned and influenced by big business have been tireless in their defence of this detachment by corporations from any social obligations. In the new global economy, they tell us, companies must be free to move their operations anywhere in the world if that is what it takes to reduce costs and maximize returns to their shareholders. That is the key to survival in the global business jungle, the right-wing editorial writers and columnists repeatedly argue. There is no longer any room for social sentimentality, especially if it cuts into profits.

How successful have the apologists for corporate irresponsibility been in convincing people that such neglect of community well-being is justified? Well, clearly the majority have been duped. They still accept the "need" for—or "unavoidability" of—mass layoffs, tax-dodging, and plant relocations. It may seem that the glib excuses repeatedly drummed into us—globalization, international competition and free trade—have had the desired effect on public opinion.

Recently, however, we have seen evidence that, while a majority continue to swallow the corporate line, a surprisingly large minority have come to reject it. This was revealed in a recent international poll by Environics.

You probably never saw this poll, since, not surprisingly, it was either ignored by the mainstream media or buried on a back page of the business section.

Environics asked more than 25,000 people in 23 countries if they believed that corporations should be responsible for setting "higher ethical standards and helping to build a better society for all." Of the 1,500 Canadians polled, a stunning 43% said Yes. Only Australia, with 45%, had a higher percentage favouring greater corporate responsibility. As might be expected, only 35% of Americans felt that way.

Doug Miller, president of Environics International Ltd., says that Canadians are among the global leaders in judging companies on how they treat their employees, interact with the environment, and plow back some of their profits into the community.

"Our research," he says, "shows that half of Canadians last year punished a company they felt was not as socially responsible as it should be—either by avoiding its products or services, or by speaking negatively against it." Nike, for example, lost 30% of its sales within two months after its use of child labour was exposed.

Barely 11% of Canadians said that corporations should only be responsible for making money, paying their taxes, and obeying laws.

We shouldn't interpret the results of this poll as a wide-spread public revolt against the corporate agenda. At most, it shows a growing tendency to question corporate propaganda and the specious rationale for putting profits before people. Still, it is a very welcome development. It may even reflect some measure of success by progressive institutions (such as, ahem, the CCPA) in their efforts to develop and popularize more socially beneficial economic policies.

It will take a lot more work, however, before the concept of good corporate citizenship becomes a reality instead of a myth.❖

PART VI

Corporate Rule: Challenged

The revolt against corporate rule
Tips on taming the TNCs
Barbarism, Inc.
The right to strike
Harnessing our power as consumers
Why we need our own media
The fate of the modern heretic
It all boils down to unfair distribution

The revolt against corporate rule

When I first started writing about the corporate takeover of our economic and political systems about 25 years ago, I didn't have much company. Most people, even some of my close associates, considered me a crackpot, at least on this particular subject. It wasn't fashionable, back then, to question the motives and morals of large corporations.

Today, however, I find myself part of a growing chorus of dissent. Critics of corporate behaviour are popping up all over the place, even, occasionally, in such bastions of the commercial press as *The Wall Street Journal, Time, The New York Times,* and *Business Week.*

Also proliferating around the world are community-based groups and coalitions committed to challenging corporate rule. There are literally thousands of them now, many with their own publications and web-sites, and they are increasingly linking up, via the Internet, to work together on global projects—and even to come together in large numbers, physically, as they did for the "battle of Seattle" late last year.

The fights against the MAI and the WTO's Millennium Round were won (or perhaps "stalled" would be more accurate) through the "early-warning" system set up by this network, by the sharing of vital information and the pooling of resources. Granted, it was the pull-out from the MAI talks by the government of France that finally forced the corporations to abandon their effort to finesse this bill of corporate rights through the OECD. But it was the activist groups that first alerted the French (and everyone else) to the MAI's planned entrenchment of corporate rights on a global basis.

The corporations themselves have also, if unwittingly, helped to expose their own depredations. When their "free market" forays spread unemployment to 30% of the world's

labour force, when the money-traders wreck national economies, when social programs are slashed to pay crushing debt
loads, when poverty and hunger and preventable disease afflict many more millions, when the toxic wastes spewed from
factories poison the environment and threaten life itself—then
it becomes very difficult for the corporations and their media
and academic apologists to disclaim responsibility. Even the
least educated and analytical of their victims can now identify the corporations as the source of their problems.

Unfortunately, this growing public awareness cannot easily be harnessed to an effective campaign to overthrow our
corporate rulers. Wealth and the power it bestows remain
concentrated in their hands. All the major political parties,
willingly or through intimidation, remain subservient to them.
There is, in short, no means readily available to bring the corporations to heel, or to seriously obstruct their devastating
proclivities.

Of course, if people become so destitute and desperate
that they have nothing more to lose, they will sometimes resort to violence. Witness the widespread rioting in Indonesia, South Korea, and other countries in Asia victimized by
Western financial speculators. Witness (on a much smaller
scale) the sabotaging of oil companies in Alberta whose emissions have hurt farmers and their crops and livestock.

As a corrective measure, however, violent and illegal acts
can't be condoned, no matter how extreme the provocation.
Nor is there much of a constituency for this sort of thing in
the Western world—although the French and other Europe-
ans are certainly not averse to taking to the streets *en masse* if
they are outraged by some government or business policy.

The two scenarios now being advanced are that 1) the
whole global corporate free market structure will eventually
come crashing down, demolished by its own internal strains

and excesses, or 2) the CEOs will come to their senses in time to humanize and thus preserve their New World Order.

The second scenario, in my view, is the more likely. But it will do no more than apply Band-aids to the worst social and economic wounds the corporations have inflicted. Unemployment may ease up, the poor may be made less poor, and income disparities may be narrowed. The CEOs may even submit to having some semblance of regulatory control applied to their most ruthless practices. But nothing of any importance will change. The corporations will continue to run the world, if on a slightly less arrogant and reckless scale.

This is because there are no longer any constraints on corporate conduct in our laws and constitutions. The corporations rule—instead of democratically elected governments—because they have been given the right to do so. And because most people today assume (quite wrongly) that the corporations have always had this right.

It's not generally known that, when the first corporations were set up, centuries ago, they had none of the power and privilege they now enjoy. They were kept on a very short leash. They had to obtain charters from governments which spelled out their limited rights. They were not allowed to participate in politics or education or any other activity not directly tied to their business. A corporation that strayed beyond the narrow scope of its charter, or did anything that was viewed as harmful to the public interest, had its charter revoked and was dissolved. In short, the people (through their elected representatives) controlled the corporations.

How did that relationship get reversed? It's a long story, but basically what happened was that, in the latter half of the 1800s, the corporations were able to use their growing wealth to influence (a.k.a., buy) large numbers of politicians and judges. The result was a series of legal amendments and rulings that greatly expanded the freedom of the corporations.

The most significant was the decision to give corporations the right of "personhood," which meant their non-business activities could no longer be prohibited. They were set free to extend their power into the political process, into education, into the purchase of newspapers and radio stations, into any other sphere into which individual citizens were allowed to venture.

One of the first victories of the newly empowered corporations was to escape from the limits and accountability built into their charters. They couldn't openly demand that they be freed entirely from government restraints, so they devised the bright idea of having their activities "regulated" and inspected. They knew that most of the ensuing regulations would be weakly enforced, if at all, and so could be ignored with impunity. In the unlikely event that they were ever caught price-gouging or producing defective products or dumping toxic waste into the rivers (and actually convicted), they would only have to pay a token fine and then could resume their illegal practices.

Freed from effective public control, the corporations grew in size and wealth and power, and inevitably became the dominant organizations in the world. As a result, democracy has given way to a corporate oligarchy.

The corporate oligarchs, however, are not so securely enthroned that they can't be dethroned. Quite aside from the internal problems they're having with the shaky global system they've created, they have not proved invulnerable to public opposition when it is properly and strategically focused. Some of the skirmishes (not just the anti-MAI clash) have gone against them.

As Richard Grossman of POCLAD has pointed out, however, despite many successful campaigns by those who seek to restore true democracy, "the imperial corporations remain." Their rule has not yet been seriously challenged. They can afford to lose some encounters with civil society groups and still preserve their supremacy.

Grossman is on the right track when he calls on the pro-democracy forces to start attacking the corporations at their weakest point, which is still—even if now just nominally—the charters that give them their right to exist.

These charters now are granted in perpetuity, contain few obligations or constraints, and are only technically subject to government review. Their wording, however, could be changed to incorporate limits and penalties comparable to those that were included in the business charters of the past. They could be denied the protection of limited liability, prohibited from participating in elections and public policy, kicked out of the schools and anywhere else they intruded.

Of course, these much-needed amendments could only be enacted by governments that served the people rather than the corporations. And, unfortunately, very few such governments can be found anywhere in the world today at the national level. The vast majority have been co-opted or coerced by big business. At the regional and local levels, however, politicians can still be found who are both willing and able to get tough with misbehaving business firms.

Three recent examples from the United States—the bastion of corporate power—may suffice to make this point.

1. The town council of Wayne, Pennsylvania, enacted a new law in 1998 aimed at corporations found guilty of violating labour, environmental, health and safety, or tax and consumer regulations. Such corporations are now prohbited from doing business in the town.

2. Citizens of the city of Arcata, California, voted by a 61% majority to set up a Commission on Democracy and Corporations that will monitor all companies doing business in the city, with a view to banning any of their practices that harm

or threaten the well-being of the citizens and their environment.

3. The Attorney-General of the state of New York, Dennis Vacco, has revoked the charter of an agency that fronted for the big tobacco companies: the Council for Tobacco Research. He accused it of posing as a non-profit organization, while feeding the public "a pack of lies in an underhanded effort to promote smoking and addict our kids." The assets of the now-dissolved council have been turned over to the Health Sciences Centre at the State University of New York in Buffalo.

We shouldn't read too much into these isolated incidents. I would have been much more impressed, for example, if Vacco had revoked the charter of Philip-Morris or Rothmans instead of one of the tobacco giants' front groups. But such developments do reflect, I think, a greater willingness to tackle corporate power at the regional and local levels.

The same trend is evident in the decision by several municipalities and universities (in Canada as well as the U.S.) to declare themselves "sweatshop-free zones" by refusing to purchase goods made in countries that underpay and mistreat their workers. The City of Ottawa even rejected a grant from Nike to improve a city gym because of the company's exploitation of cheap foreign labour.

The most effective curbs against corporate pollution are also emanating from municipal and regional governments (perhaps because they are closer and more accessible to the people) rather than from federal and provincial politicians.

As the campaign against corporate rule gains momentum, it may therefore be advisable to "think globally, but act locally." Actions taken at the community level—particularly those that challenge the legal and constitutional legitimacy of corporate "rights"—may not have the same headline-grabbing impact that a national or international project could, but they are the most promising in terms of mustering public support and participation.

And they set the examples and precedents that the broader movement against corporate rule needs to build on in the years ahead.❖

Tips on taming the TNCs

One of the knocks against my columns is that they go on at length (some might say *ad nauseam*) about how powerful and ruthless and destructive the transnational corporations are, without offering much advice on how to challenge and eventually control them.

This is not entirely true. I've devoted several columns to fight-back tactics, from tapping union pension power to establishing our own media. It might be helpful, however, to summarize the various ways in which Canadians, either as individuals or working together, could work effectively to curb the TNCs' power. I list them in the order of their feasibility, as I rate them.

1. Spread the word. The main reason I keep talking about the TNCs' economic and political domination is because the general public still remains oblivious. The iconoclastic U.S. film-maker and author Michael Moore claims that most people are already aware that the TNCs are in control, and in that respect are ahead of the left's leaders. On that point I disagree. It's true that they resent being laid off or having their wages decline, but the vast majority still don't know they live under corporate rule, and that most of their problems stem from an out-of-control "free market" system. Unless they understand that, they can hardly be expected to join or support efforts to restore true democracy.

That's why I continue to urge leaders of unions and other NGOs to give top priority to informing and enlightening the public, starting with their own rank-and-file members. This is a *sine-qua-non*. It's not "preaching to the converted," because, believe me, most of those who would be on our side if they were fully informed still lack the basic knowledge.

It would be great to have our own national media to help spread the message, as I have also rather naively proposed, but it's not essential. What is essential is a decision to undertake this educational campaign by whatever means are available (e.g., newsletters, the Internet, meetings, even door-to-door canvassing), and to devote the necessary resources to it. We have to keep in mind that the members of our various organizations, along with their families, comprise a good chunk of the "public"—maybe as many as half—and their enlightenment would inevitably spread through the general populace.

2. Become self-reliant. The big corporations aren't as dependent on us as consumers as they used to be, but they still want us to buy their goods and services—maybe even more so now that the economic crisis in Southeast Asia has sharply curtailed their sales in that region. To the extent that we can do without the TNCs and their products, or at least minimize our consumption, to that extent we loosen their economic grip on us.

At the community level, this means making our local economy as self-reliant as possible, producing as many of our own needs as we can. This is basically what the "sustainable economy" movement is all about. It can take many forms, ranging from promoting the three R's—reducing, reusing and recycling—to patronizing local producers and service providers.

It can also involve the creation of a local currency. Some cities and towns have already introduced what is called a

Local Employment and Trading System (LETS), which involves the use of local "money" in buying and selling within the community. It has the advantage of avoiding (legally) the payment of both interest and taxes, while thumbing your nose at the big banks—perhaps the biggest reward of all.

3. Boycott the worst TNCs (and the countries that harbour them). Nearly half the merchandise in our stores these days comes from sweatshop labour, child labour, prison labour and even slave labour. If you don't believe me, look at the labels. Every time we buy one of these items, we are helping to increase the profits of companies that grossly underpay, overwork and mistreat their workers. We are helping to entrench this exploitation of our fellow human beings abroad, helping to destroy the jobs of our fellow citizens at home, and of course helping to perpetuate global corporate rule.

Now, I know it's difficult to find products that don't come from sweated labour, and that, when we do find them, they usually cost more—more, even, than many low-income people can afford. But as our jobs disappear and our wages decline, if we react by buying the cheapest foreign-made goods, we eliminate more jobs in Canada and drive our wages even lower.

Breaking out of this vicious circle requires some sacrifice, and it may be a sacrifice many of us can no longer make. But at least we can all be more selective as consumers. If we feel we have no choice but to buy a serf-labour product, let's not buy one made by the TNCs with the worst labour practices. And if there are any TNCs that treat their Third World workers fairly, or even less harshly (don't ask me to name one), let's favour them at the check-out counters.

4. Use workers' financial power to curb the TNCs' financial power. This, of course, means gaining some control over the $500 billion in workers' pension funds, and over how these vast sums are managed and invested. In a system where money is power, and vice versa, the TNCs—particularly the big financial institutions—can only be confronted on anything like a level playing field if the groups opposing them wield strong financial weapons of their own.

I'm well aware that this is a lot easier to say than do. There are complex legal and regulatory barriers to overcome, having to do with pension trustees' "fiduciary responsibility" and other constraints. But they're not insurmountable. What's missing in Canada, so far, is the will even to make the attempt to harness this potential resource in the struggle against corporate rule. (It's encouraging, however, to see that the labour movement in the U.S. is moving to deploy this powerful financial weapon on behalf of workers in that country.)

5. Elect governments of, by and for the people. I put this option low on my list because I see little hope of its happening unless some of the previous measures are first successful—especially the creation of an informed electorate. As long as the TNCs can continue to co-opt or coerce the politicians and bamboozle most of the voters, we'll continue to have a system of plutocracy in Canada, instead of democracy, and the corporate agenda will continue to be the only one pursued in our legislatures.

Only if the TNCs can be brought to heel by the emergence of a community-based "citizens' politics" will there be any chance of electing a government that puts people ahead of profiteers. Only then will there be any hope of having the TNCs' power civilized once again by fully-enforced laws, regulations and standards. Only then will the TNCs be held accountable for their practices that affect their employees, their customers, and the environment. Only then will they be compelled to pay their fair share of taxes. Those among us who have a bent for "political action" are wasting their time if they keep trying to achieve needed reforms within the undemocratic system that now prevails. Even worse, they are acting as if they believe we still have a real democracy, and thus indirectly are discouraging efforts to restore it. Better by far that they divert their activism into one or more of the worthwhile endeavours previously listed.

6. Wait for the New Corporate World Order to self-destruct. This is not a serious option, of course, but you'd be surprised how many people on the left think it is. They point to all the flaws and failings of the global economy under the TNCs—including the recent financial "meltdowns" in Southeast Asia—and confidently predict that the whole globalized system will sooner or later come crashing down, a victim of its own internal strains and stresses.

I don't dismiss this possibility altogether, but I doubt if the business leaders who run the global economy are dumb enough to let it collapse. They have a strong survival instinct, and a record of adapting quickly to changing circumstances. In any case, as long as they can control the politicians and con the voters, why should they worry if their uncontrolled greed sometimes backfires on them? They can always count on their puppet governments to use taxpayers' money to bail them out, as is happening in Asia today, and previously in the peso crisis in Mexico, in the savings and loans fiasco in the U.S., and in the real estate collapse of the 1980s in Canada.

If you or I were to lose money gambling or investing unwisely, that would be our tough luck. But if you're the CEO of a big corporation or bank and you lose billions betting on bad loans or investing in shaky stock deals, you can count on governments to come galloping to your rescue. So how can a system fail when the TNCs' political servants won't let it fail?—when they are prepared to loot billions from the public treasury for business bailouts? (And without, I might add, any cries of outrage from the taxpayers whose pockets are thus being so blatantly picked.)

So let's not rely on the TNCs to become the victims of their own greed or incompetence. Sure, there will be the occasional crisis in some industry or region, but with all the economic and political structures committed to preventing a general breakdown of the "free market" system, it's not going to occur without a great deal of public pressure.

We're going to have to work at it.

I don't pretend to have cited all the methods that could be tried to expose, confront and eventually topple our corporate rulers. I do think that the process, essentially, has to be a bottom-up one, starting first with individual awareness and motivation, then extending to the community level, then to the national and ultimately the world stage.

In terms of collective action, we already have a lot of NGOs that can participate in the struggle (and to some extent already are). They include social action coalitions, unions, women's groups, churches, environmental groups, consumer watchdogs, anti-poverty groups, and at least a few progressive research agencies. What they lack at present is the ability to work together, to pool their resources. As long as they all concentrate on their own specific areas of concern, instead of cooperating against the common enemy and for a common goal, their overall efforts will continue to be stymied.

Ever the optimist, I wait patiently for this great united fire brigade to materialize and aim its hoses at the worst social and economic conflagrations. But, while I'm waiting, I'll keep sounding the fire alarm and pointing frantically to the arsonists. And if that means that I'm considered too "alarmist," or too "negative," or too "paranoid," or even too "idealistic," that's a price the bearer of bad news must sometimes pay.

Maybe, eventually, more people will decide to listen to the messsage, and act on it, instead of wanting to shoot the messenger.❖

Barbarianism, Inc.

Occasionally, when I venture beyond the friendly confines of the left, I am accosted by people who don't share my aversion for the big corporations and their CEOs.

"What have you got against capitalism?" I am asked, accusingly. Sometimes there's a follow-up query: "Would you rather live under a communist system?"

To the first question, my flip response is usually that I can't spare the hours or days it would take to list all my objections to the New World Order; and to the second I aver that the choice is not between capitalism and communism, per se, but between civilized and uncivilized ways to run an economy. Capitalism as it is practised today is clearly no improvement over Soviet communism, and arguably is even worse for the majority of people who live under it.

Come to think of it, I could sum up all my reasons for loathing free-market capitalism in just three words: *it is barbaric.*

Look up the word "barbaric" in your dictionary, and you'll find several synonyms, including brutal, savage, and cruel. They all apply to the current capitalist system—and even more so to its overlords. These suave chief executives don't look or act like Attila the Hun. They dress smartly, talk smoothly, and their table manners are impeccable. But strip away the glossy veneer, and you find the savage, ruthless tyrants not far beneath the surface.

These modern barbarian chieftains don't personally lead their hordes to invade other countries. They don't physically destroy cultures. They don't openly loot and pillage cities, or massacre their inhabitants. But they engage in the equivalent of all these barbaric activities from the seclusion of their boardrooms, sometimes with just a phone call or a tap on a computer key.

Their invasions take the form of "free trade." Their looting and pillaging is done through strip-mining, deforestation, privatization and deregulation, currency speculation, and IMF-enforced repayments of onerous debt-loads.

In the wake of these corporate depredations, billions of people are doomed to poverty, hunger and disease, and many thousands to premature death. They are as much the victims of barbarism as were those slaughtered by Attila and Genghis Khan. The business brigands who plan and direct these pogroms don't have blood on their well-manicured hands, but they make the Goths and Vandals look like teenaged delinquents.

What do I have against capitalism, indeed! Am I supposed to applaud and endorse an economic system in which 225 billionaires have more money than the two billion poorest people? In which just 4% of the wealth of those 225 individuals—about $40 billion a year—would be enough to eliminate world hunger and provide adequate health care and basic education for everyone?

Sorry, but I don't buy all the glib excuses and rationalizations for this obscenely inhumane system trotted out by the élites and their propagandists. "The poor will always be with us," they say, quoting the bible. (Yes, they certainly will be as long as the God of the Market so decrees.) "You can't help the poor, sick and hungry by throwing money at them." (How about not taking the money away from them in the first place?)

For me, the two events in 1998 that most tellingly revealed the true face of modern capitalism were the crisis on Wall Street in September and the crisis in Central America in November.

The crisis on Wall Street was the imminent collapse of a major investment fund—Long-Term Capital Management—after it lost billions gambling on the rise or fall of European currencies. The fund's affluent managers and several hundred investors (who had no one to blame except their own avarice) cried out to be rescued from their folly, and it took just a few days to accumulate the $3.5 billion needed to bail out their fund.

The crisis in Honduras, Guatemala, Nicaragua and El Salvador ravaged millions of people in those countries whose lives and economies were shattered by Hurricane Mitch. But these were not rich investors or speculators. They were poor, homeless, hungry members of the lower classes. So the Chrétien government's first response was to offer them a paltry $1 million in aid, while the U.S. government coughed up $2 million.

Only public outrage over these meagre amounts forced the two governments to increase them. Eventually, with the help of other nations in Europe, the total aid package was boosted to half-a-billion, but this still fell far short of the $2 billion or more needed by Mitch's helpless victims—and well short of the amount raised almost overnight for the wealthy Wall Street speculators.

The lesson is that there is fast and generous charity for the greedy, slow and grudging charity for the needy.

Basically, capitalism enshrines greed—one of the most repugnant of human vices—as the predominant virtue. The whole system is driven by greed. Selfishness harnessed to initiative is supposed to produce the best of all ways to run an economy, or a country—or even the world.

The truth, of course, is that any system that enshrines rapacity as its motivating force must by its very nature be a form of barbarism.

Is this really the best system that humankind can devise to allocate the planet's resources? If so, we have no right to call our society civilized. (Or our species, either.) It is just as primitive and causes as much misery and injustice as any social or economic system in human history. A good case could even be made, now that the corporations have succeeded in dominating the entire planet, that this is by far the most unjust and brutal system ever to oppress the world's people.

Its defenders argue that it simply reflects the reality of Nature, "red in tooth and claw," which dictates that the law of the jungle must also be the overriding law governing human affairs. All creatures, they claim, are either predators or prey, and the struggle to survive must play itself out in the human jungle, too.

If that were true, however, the human predators would not take more prey than they need to survive. The lions and tigers aren't greedy. They don't keep killing more zebras and antelope than they can eat. There aren't 225 lions with more to eat than two billion hogs or deer or giraffes.

So don't prattle to me about the law of the jungle or the survival of the fittest. That's an insult to the animals. What we have is an economic system that glorifies, promotes and rewards the basest of human instincts—a system that carries cruelty, injustice and brutalization to their worst extremes.❖

The right to strike

"Workers' complaints multiplied, and strikes grew more frequent—strikes among the miners, the tradesmen, even among the police."

A description of the mounting labour relations conflict in Canada in 1999? No, it's historian W. W. Tarn's account of the economic problems of Egypt in 230 B.C.

According to Tarn, the first recorded strikes in history were conducted by workers on the great pyramids of Egypt many thousands of years earlier.

References to strikes have been found on the papayri and tablets of ancient Persia, Sumeria, and other long-vanished civilizations.

The Roman Empire experienced numerous strikes by coppersmiths, goldsmiths, shoemakers, potters, dyers and carpenters.

In the industrial towns of France and Italy in the 13th and 14th centuries, the craft guilds went on strike repeatedly against the ruling merchant class. Textile workers at Rouen staged a lengthy strike in 1281. Woolworkers in France went on strike in 1371.

Strikes occurred in England as early as the 1300s, with a contemporary writer complaining that even priests had struck for higher pay.

In their monumental *Story of Civilization*, Will and Ariel Durant tell us that in 1579 textile workers went on strike in Germany, and that throughout the 16th century in Europe "strikes were numerous, but they were suppressed by a coalition of employers and governments." (Who says history doesn't repeat itself?)

Major strikes also took place in the factories of Amsterdam in 1672, and in the silk-making plants of Lyons in 1774.

This brief history lesson is for the benefit of those present-day Canadians who seem to believe that the strike is a diabolical invention of modern unions.

These are the people who keep urging, in letters to the editor and on radio hot-line shows, that unions be stripped of their right to strike—especially unions in the public sector. They seem to believe that simply outlawing strikes would ensure "labour peace"—that all forms of labour-management conflict would then suddenly disappear.

What would happen instead would be chaos, not peace. Strikes would proliferate, not diminish, even if they were made illegal.

We should learn from the lessons of the past. There has never been a period in human history that was entirely free of strikes, ever since some people were obliged to work for others. The relationship between workers and their bosses almost inevitably breeds resentment and conflict. And when their discontent rises to an intolerable level, workers will strike—whether they have unions or not, and regardless, too, of the kind of political and economic system in which they live.

Most of the strikes of bygone eras occurred under totalitarian regimes that prohibited strikes and ruthlessly quelled them. Strikers were severely punished, their leaders hanged or beheaded.

Not even such harsh deterrents, however, could prevent strikes. They have continued to erupt down through the ages.

It is important, when looking at the growing incidence of strikes in Canada today—most of them provoked by corporate arrogance or government cutbacks—to keep them in historical perspective, and to realize that strikes predated modern unions by more than 8,000 years.

The first recorded strike in what was to become Canada, for example, took place when the voyageurs at Rainy Lake went on strike for higher wages in August of 1794, more than half a century before the first union made its appearance here.

The evidence is clear, for those open-minded enough to see it, that unions do not instigate labour strife—that instead they do their utmost to avert it.

Economist John Kenneth Galbraith calls unions "managers of discontent," in the sense that they serve as a vehicle for resolving workers' grievances—and thus in most cases preventing their escalation into work stoppages.

"The clauses in unions' collective agreements that regulate pay, benefits, seniority, and conditions of promotion are voluminous," Galbraith points out. "Any unilaterial application of such rules by management, however meticulous, would seem arbitrary and unjust. By helping to frame the rules and by participating in the grievance machinery, the union serves invaluably to mitigate the feeling (among workers) that such systems are unfair."

No union ever stages a strike from whim or malice, or with the idea that a strike would somehow be preferable to a mutually satisfactory agreement. The reverse is true. Unions regard strikes as costly and troublesome, and make every effort to avoid them. When they do call a strike, it is only as a last resort, after all atempts to negotiate a peaceful settlement have failed, or when they have been backed into a corner by an intransigent employer or an anti-union government.

So effective are unions in averting strikes that they have been accused by some left-wing critics of acting as enforcers of labour peace on behalf of employers.

In his book *Strike,* for example, Jeremy Brecher claims that the function of unions today "is to set the terms on which workers will submit to the managers' authority . . . Once employers accept a contract, the jobs of union officials depend on their enforcement of the contract—that is, preventing strikes."

A more balanced view, by economist J. Raymond Walsh, is that "union leaders, far from fomenting trouble, spend most of their time settling disputes before the strike stage is reached."

The underlying reality is that conflict is built into our private enterprise system. It is a system in which workers can only get more if their employers take less, a system in which both sides are continually at odds over how revenue is to be shared among them.

In such an inherently adversarial system, the wonder is not that there are so many strikes, but that there are so few.

Without unions to represent workers and channel their anger and frustration constructively through collective bargaining, the workplace would fall into anarchy. Strikes would become much more frequent, and workers would resort to more damaging forms of protest, such as working to rule, slowdowns, sit-ins, mass absenteeism, and even outright sabotage.

Instead of trying to hobble or even get rid of unions, those who yearn for a labour relations paradise should be thankful that unions exist. They should hail the unions' success—despite the growing hostility of employers and governments—in still managing to settle 95 out of 100 contract negotiations without a strike.❖

A plug for "Silent Coup"

"Don't buy a single vote more than necessary. I'll be damned if I'm going to pay for a landslide."
—Joseph Kennedy, U.S. businessman, in a
telegram to his son, presidential
candidate John F. Kennedy, 1960.

Canada's business executives obviously didn't want to pay for another landslide by Jean Chrétien, either, in 1997. But of course they don't really care which party forms the federal government. They knew that, no matter how the seating arrangements in the House of Commons were reshuffled by the 1997 "election," the only real winners would be them—the CEOs who secretly control all our governments.

They knew that the corporate agenda would continue to be followed, because all but a few of the elected and re-elected MPs—regardless of party affiliation—would be committed to it. The great majority would still favour more social pro-

gram cuts, privatization, deregulation, more foreign investment, more free trade, lower business taxes, lower wages—
all the policies, in short, that favour the transnational corporations (TNCs) at everyone else's expense.

The CEOs knew that, whatever the composition of the
next Parliament, it would do their bidding. It would push
through the extension of free trade into Central and South
America to exploit the cheap labour in those countries. It
would continue to promote through APEC more business
deals with the brutal military regimes in Asia. It would do its
best to ram through the Multilateral Agreement on Investments that, if adopted, would remove the last vestiges of true
democracy in Canada.

All of these moves to consolidate the power and privilege
of the TNCs would be implemented by whatever bunch of
politicians happened to occupy the government seats because
big business has taken over our political system as well as
our economy.

Unfortunately, only about one Canadian in a thousand is
even aware that this coup d'état has occurred. Most still believe they can change government policies by changing governments. They still believe they live in a genuine democracy
in which the political candidates they elect will be responsive to their needs and concerns.

If they don't soon wake up to the reality of corporate rule,
it may be too late to stop the complete conversion of Canada
into a puppet state of the TNCs. Thankfully, this wake-up
call has now come, in the form of a new and riveting book by
social activist Tony Clarke.

In *"Silent Coup: Confronting the Big Business Takeover of
Canada,"* Clarke not only outlines the 20-year plan devised
by the business barons to seize power. He also maps out a
detailed strategy for restoring democracy and derailing the
corporate agenda.

The first and most difficult task he attempts is to convince people that there really was a silent and surreptitious coup, and that we are now living under the equivalent of a corporate dictatorship. For most Canadians, that will be an enormous mental leap. The corporate coup d'état has been so insidious, so cleverly concealed behind the facade of democracy, that it remains undetected by the average person. It is visible only through its consequences—through the adoption of economic and social policies beneficial only to the TNCs: policies obsequiously justified by their academic and media minions, and dutifully delivered by their political servants.

Clarke's book was of course attacked and ridiculed by these same corporate Quislings. They tried to dismiss him as a crazy conspiracy theorist. They ridiculed his book as an exercise in paranoia. And these attacks probably had the desired effect of dissuading many Canadians from reading "Silent Coup."

Those who refuse to be so deluded, however, will be richly rewarded by this book. It has the potential to be a catalyst—a turning-point in the so-far futile struggle against corporate rule. Far from being a rhetorical rant, it is a well-documented, fact-filled, clearly written exposé of the corporate takeover—how and why it happened, who the major players and collaborators were, and what grim results it produced and still has in store for us.

Armed with this information, readers of "Silent Coup" will be as angry as they are enlightened. They will want to get involved in the fight against corporate rule. And Clarke obligingly gives them the tools and the strategy they need to undertake this formidable task. This is the strength of his book. It doesn't stop at exposing the big business takeover. It tells us how to go about undoing it.

Realistically, of course, most Canadians will never read "Silent Coup." Its publishers don't have the resources to promote it extensively, and the harshly negative reviews from the corporate media predictably have kept it off the best-seller lists. But even if the book's readers number only five or ten thousand, to that extent at least the knowledge of the business takeover will be spread. To that extent the seeds of a popular revolt will be sown.

"The longest journey," the Chinese proverb reminds us, "begins with a single step." The first step on the long journey back to a democratic Canada begins with reading *"Silent Coup."*❖

Harnessing our power as consumers

The clothing racks in Canadian stores are now so crammed with apparel made in Third World sweatshops that it's becoming difficult to find shirts, sweaters, pants and jackets that are made in Canada. The same is true for footwear, and even many household appliances.

Most Canadians, unfortunately, don't even make the effort to find domestic products. They're happy to buy the clothing sewn by grossly underpaid and mistreated workers in Haiti, Guatemala, Burma, Malaysia, and other countries where slave labour, prison labour and child labour are rampant.

The outfits imported from Asia and Latin America are usually much cheaper than comparable garments made in Canada by workers who are unionized and therefore paid decent wages. Even our non-unionized clothing workers are far better compensated than those in most developing nations.

Most of us, however, remain oblivious to the atrocious working conditions and indecently low wages being enforced on millions of workers outside Canada, many of them young children. (The United Nations calculates that the children aged five to 14 now employed in the Third World number at least 250 million.)

In Burma, grossly underpaid workers suppressed by a brutal military regime sew Mickey Mouse shirts for the Walt Disney company. In China, young peasant women work 12-hour shifts for 25 cents an hour assembling Nike and Reebok athletic shoes.

The mistreatment of so many workers in the Third World should be a matter of more concern in Canada. Not just because we want to help them, but because we want to help ourselves. Their exploitation is part of a vast global strategy designed ultimately to force wages down to bare subsistence levels in Canada and other "developed" nations, as well.

This strategy is already far advanced. Freed from national restrictions by free trade, deregulation, and the new communications technologies, the transnational corporations (TNCs) can now relocate production to the countries and regions that offer the cheapest labour—and the weakest labour laws. So jobs by the hundreds of thousands are being shifted from Canada and other "high-wage" countries to the factories that use child labour, prison labour and serf labour in Southeast Asia and Latin America.

Canadian workers and their unions have been powerless to stop this exodus of jobs. It is having its intended effect of raising unemployment and lowering Canadian workers' real wages—and thus making cheap foreign-made products more attractive to us.

As consumers, however, we are far from powerless to oppose the second stage of the TNCs' low-wage strategy. We can refuse to buy the products of their Third World sweatshops. In the short term, that may increase our living expenses, but in the long term it may save our jobs and prevent our wages from going into free fall.

The corporations are counting on us to keep our needs as consumers entirely separate from our needs as workers. They are confident we'll continue to buy the clothing made in China and Haiti, buy the shoes made in China and Indonesia, buy the electronic devices made in Malaysia. And, unfortunately, up to now, most of us have done just that. As consumers, we instinctively look for the best bargains, for the goods that take the least out of our tight household budgets, regardless of where they're produced.

If we stopped to think, however, we would realize that, by purchasing the products of cheap, sweated labour in the Third World, we are unthinkingly worsening our own financial insecurity. The more of such products we purchase, the more we reward the TNCs for their downsizing here and their cheap labour strategy abroad. And we don't do any favours to the exploited foreign workers, either. We are in effect perpetuating their serfdom.

Right-wing politicians, business leaders and academics argue that, if we boycotted goods made by underpaid foreign workers, we would be depriving them of their only means of livelihood, as inadequate as it may be. This claim is as spurious today as it was in Victorian times when it was used to rationalize the use of child labour. ("Take away these kids' jobs, and they'll starve to death or turn to lives of crime.")

The same flawed argument was trotted out by the neo-cons to oppose the economic boycott of South Africa. Had their protests been heeded, that country would still be ruled by a racist, oppressive government that discriminated against the majority of its population. Without the economic sanctions that were imposed on South Africa, the enforcers of apartheid would still be in power there. Nelson Mandela would still be in jail instead of having the privilege of heading the country's government.

The leaders of opposition movements in developing nations ruled by dictators know that boycotts of sweatshop goods would temporarily add to their people's hardship. But they also know that such boycotts offer the best hope of toppling the dictators and thereby improving their people's lives. That's why they would endorse, not condemn, a concerted effort on our part to stop buying the products of the TNCs' slave-labour factories.

The leader of Burma's National League for Democracy, Nobel Prize winner Aung San Suu Kyi, faces the same uphill struggle today that Mandela and his supporters faced in South Africa. She, too, was jailed by Burma's ruthless military rulers, and still endures their harassment. She favours the same kind of economic sanctions that finally got rid of apartheid in South Africa, even if they temporarily result in more hardship for Burmese workers.

"All profits from business enterprises in my country," she said recently, "go to a small, privileged elite. Companies that continue to invest here only serve to prolong the agony of my country by encouraging the military regime to persevere in its atrocities."

She could have said the same thing about consumers in Canada and other developed nations who also prop up the Burmese dictators by buying made-in-Burma merchandise.

It's time for us to look at the labels on the goods we buy. We would accomplish three desirable objectives if we decided from now on to "shop Canadian"—or at least to "shop non-sweatshop." 1) We would be helping to slow down and eventually stop the export of jobs from Canada, and perhaps even repatriate some of those already lost. 2) We would be helping our counterparts in the developing nations to throw off the yoke of military and corporate tyranny. And 3) we would be effectively challenging the TNCs' global low-wage strategy.

Admittedly, such a boycott would involve some additional costs to us as consumers. But these costs would eventually be more than offset by the gains we would derive as workers—and the gains that would be made by exploited workers in the Third World.❖

Why we need our own media

"Freedom of the press is guaranteed only to those who own one."
—A. J. Liebling.

"We have the press we deserve, not the press we need."
—Senator Keith Davey.

"The *Globe and Mail* tells you what to think every morning. You get up, go to the refrigerator and get out that nice cold orange juice. Then you have a very hot coffee on top of that. And the *Globe and Mail* editorial on top of that. Then you have a bowel movement. It is truly extraordinary."
—Patrick McFadden, professor of journalism, Carleton University.

If I wanted to add one of my own quotes, it would be that "our corporate rulers don't need concentration camps to imprison our bodies so long as they have the media apparatus to imprison our minds."

I've been trying for many years to convince the various groups on the left (and their leaders) that the most important war they are now fighting—or should be fighting—is a war of words. It's a contest for the minds and hearts of the Canadian people. If we lose that war, then all our other struggles—

for jobs, for fair wages, for equality, for adequate social programs—will be futile.

None of these battles can be won solely by collective bargaining, by strikes, by demonstrations, by lobbying the politicians. Not while most Canadians have been persuaded through the "big lie" technique that all the crippling assaults on them—the mass layoffs, the rise in poverty, the underfunding of our schools and hospitals, the lavish tax breaks to business, the fire sale of public assets to private firms—are either necessary or unavoidable. And persuaded, too, that there are no viable alternatives.

Our corporate rulers own the presses. They also own the private radio and television networks, and, through their political minions, exercise effective control over the CBC as well.

They also do frequent polling to ensure that their propaganda is having the desired effect. That's why it doesn't bother them when the unions and their coalition allies—with months of time and effort—manage to get 100,000 people out for a one-day protest. They know that four out of five Canadians— including most union members—remain safely brainwashed.

No public protest will accomplish anything unless it reflects the views of the majority—or at least a sizeable minority—in which case no mobilizing effort is needed. The protest will be spontaneous, it will be massive, and it will continue for weeks or months, not just for one day. Or it will find (create) a less disruptive but no less effective political outlet.

Such a mass opposition to the ruling élite, however, can only be generated by reaching the minds of the masses first— by giving them facts instead of lies. Once people learn why and how and by whom they are being abused, they will become angry enough to rebel, and informed enough to direct their anger at their real enemies: at the corporate overlords, not the political figureheads.

Some of this educational work can be done by unions and other progressive organizations through their internal communications channels. If they did nothing else except enlighten their own members—80% of whom have swallowed the neoconservative flim-flam—they would be taking a giant step forward. (A few years ago, I drafted such a detailed internal communications program, but, as far as I know, only one labour organization has seriously tried to implement it. With, I might add, gratifying results.)

However, since most people now rely on the mass media for information, the left has no choice but to acquire its own commercial print and broadcast facilities—or greater access to the existing ones. This could necessitate buying or establishing a national newspaper and/or several regional newspapers, as well as a broadcast network or some key independent TV and radio stations. Or it could simply take the form of producing a regular paid insert in the major dailies and weeklies, and the purchase of adequate TV and radio time on an ongoing weekly basis. *[Since I first wrote this piece, the Internet has become an important medium of communication for the left, and the concept of a "virtual" alternative newspaper on the Web is now being actively explored.]*

Whenever I make this proposal—as I have, intermittently, for the past 30 years or more—the leaders of unions and other groups on the left roll their eyes derisively. They don't even consider it a serious possibility—mainly because of the huge financial outlay that would be required.

The real deterrent, however, is not financial. It's mental. The money is there—or could be raised. What's missing is the will, the imagination, the determination to confront the right-wingers on their own ideological battleground.

The unions' multi-billion-dollar pension funds are the most obvious source of the needed money. A few years ago, for example, the entire *Sun* newspaper chain could have been bought for $400 million. Not peanuts, granted, but it was roughly the amount the $50 billion Ontario teachers' pension fund accrues in interest alone every couple of months. Ironically, the professional managers of this fund, on their own, invested heavily in the purchase of the *Sun* papers, because they knew it was a safe and profitable investment. Without any control over their own fund, however, the teachers' unions had no say in this decision, and so the *Sun* papers, with the help of the teachers' pension contributions, continue serving as propaganda organs for the right—and frequently lambasting the teachers' unions in the process!

Other sources of capital that could be used to equip the left with its own media include the various labour-sponsored investment funds that have been created over the past few decades. Their total worth of about $4 billion falls far short of the $400 billion or more that have accumulated in union pension funds, but they still could potentially invest in a lot of print and broadcast business.

Even if these pension and investment funds are not tapped to finance media acquisitions, the unions could set up a separate fund for that purchase. One loonie a month from every union member in Canada, for example, would produce about $48 million a year. Not enough to challenge Conrad Black's empire, but enough to start getting serious about fighting the war of words—firing off cogent facts, figures and arguments to demolish the right's propaganda.

Still another way of funding a serious communications program would be to divert into it most of the millions of dollars now being spent (and largely wasted) by unions and other community-based organizations in ad hoc media advertising, in ineffectual house organs, in futile lobbying and demonstrations.

Some leaders on the left may doubt that, even if the money could be found to establish media outlets, they wouldn't be able to find enough objective and competent journalists to staff them. Let me put that concern to rest. There are hundreds, probably thousands, of reporters and editors toiling away for the commercial media who would love to make the switch to papers and TV and radio stations that were neither slavish mouthpieces for the corporate agenda nor flack journals for labour leaders. (One of the basic conditions for the success of a progressive newspaper or broadcasting outlet is that it must be as free from union control as corporate control.)

Media critic Walter Stewart, in his 1980 book "Canadian Newspapers: The Inside Story," said that even in one of the better newspapers, *The Toronto Star*, "all the talented reporters and superior editors are engaged, every day, in turning out a product that most of them hold in contempt."

Offer them employment where they could turn out a product they'd be proud of, and they'd jump at the chance.

Labour leaders and others on the left, however, still don't think alternative left media are the answer to the right-wing propaganda. They ask me to substantiate my belief with at least one example, and I'm only too glad to give it to them.

It was the big debate over the Charlottetown Accord. You'll recall that this formula for dismantling and decentralizing Canada was supported by every single one of the country's élite groups. Not just business leaders but also labour leaders. Not just the Liberal and Tory parties, but also the NDP. The only major groups opposed to the deal were NAC and (for its own devious reasons) the Reform Party.

Now, normally, the élites would have prevailed, particularly the corporate élite, if only because they own or control the mass media and thus can mount the most elaborate propaganda campaign, as they did in the free trade fight. But in the Charlottetown Accord fight, they miscalculated. They were so sure of their own superiority in debate and persuasion that they agreed to give the opponents of the deal equal time and space in the media.

Now, think about that. The effect was the same as if the foes of Charlottetown had their own mass media! The people of Canada, for the first time in my lifetime, got to hear both sides of a major issue in equal proportions. They truly were given the opportunity to make up their minds in full knowledge of both the pros and cons.

You know the result of the referendum. The business, political and labour establishments went down in flames. It wasn't even close. The proposed Accord was soundly rejected in nearly every region and province. As it should have been.

That was a mistake the élites never made before and unfortunately will never make again. Never again will our corporate rulers give us equal space and time in *their* media. If we want to have any chance of duplicating the Charlottetown Accord victory, we'll have to get our own media. In practical terms, there's simply no other way.

It's time to give Canadians the press they need—one that is useful for more than bowel movements.❖

The fate of the modern heretic

The brooding statue of Giordano Bruno in the Campo dei Fiori in Rome attracts few tourists. Of those who do stop to look at it, fewer still know who Bruno was and why he has been so honoured. But he is remembered in academic and literary circles, and by some modern dissidents.

This is the 400th anniversary of his death. He was a Dominican friar who quit the order to become an itinerant teacher and philosopher. He was burned at the stake for heresy by the Roman Inquisition on Feb. 17 in the year 1600.

His "heresies" were many, but the one that most angered the Vatican was a view he shared with Copernicus and Galileo that the Earth was not the centre of the universe. He wrote several treatises arguing that our planet revolves around the sun, and that the stars are distant suns that also probably have planets circling them.

This theory of course contradicted the Church's teachings that the whole universe rotates around the Earth, as God had ordained. And so Bruno was excommunicated, imprisoned for seven years, frequently tortured, and finally executed. He could perhaps have saved his life and regained his liberty if he had recanted, as Galileo did, but he refused to do so.

For his courage and his example, he has been immortalized by the statue, and he is also the character "Nolan" alluded to in James Joyce's *Finnegan's Wake*. (A Nolan is a citizen of Nola, a town near Naples, where Bruno was born.)

Novelist Morris West wrote a three-act play about Bruno, which was published as a book called *The Heretic* in 1969 and which I recently re-read. In his preface, West describes Bruno as the quintessential non-conformist of the Middle Ages, as the "odd man out" who refused to proclaim what the ruling powers (in this case the Church) insisted was true, but which he knew was false.

West wrote his play as much to honour the heretics of today as to pay homage to the historical Bruno. He said it was a mistake to assume that dissent from the prevailing orthodoxy is tolerated today any more than it was in Renaissance Italy. It's just that what West calls "the mechanics of social control" are much more sophisticated now than they were then. Heretics are not jailed, tortured or burned at the stake any more, but they are subjected to methods of suppression that can be just as effective, if not as physically painful.

"The growth in large monopolies in communication [dedicated to defending the status quo]," said West, "has forced the protester into the streets, where his protest may easily be construed or manipulated into a public disorder. A whole industry has been built around the art of affirmation, but the dignity of dissent is daily denigrated, the doubter is in disgrace...

"This is why I wrote the story of Giordano Bruno, dead and burned for heresy centuries ago. I could not believe that any man should be required to sell his soul to anyone who promised him order, discipline, social acceptance, and three meals a day."

What the Church feared 400 years ago was that Bruno's ideas and books would influence others and that a growing number of doubters and dissenters would threaten its theology and hence its power. Not having a sophisticated propaganda machine to discredit Bruno, it resorted to brute force to stop him from spreading his heretical views.

Today's ruling corporate élite also fears those who challenge its "free market" ideology, especially if they seem to be attracting a large following, but the "church" of the modern Thomas d'Aquino (no saint, he) has no need for the rack or the stake. Its version of the Inquisition is much more subtle. It attacks, refutes, ridicules and attempts to stigmatize the heretic's conflicting opinions, and thus deter their broad acceptance.

I am referring, of course, to the corporate-owned mass media, arguably the most effective mechanism for protecting a dominant doctrine that has ever been created.

Those who own and control the newspapers and the radio and TV networks are not so foolish as to try to stifle dissent completely. They allocate a limited amount of space and time for the heretics to propose different policies. This is necessary to maintain the illusion of a "free" press, but their access to the media is never enough to enable them to reach the public continuously and effectively. And their heretical views are overwhelmed by the unceasing chorus of establishment editorial writers and columnists whose main function is to disparage the dissidents and portray them as cranks and crackpots.

When a modern-day heretic still manages to garner more public support than our corporate rulers want to allow, he or she becomes the target of a more vicious and sustained smear campaign. This has been the fate of populists like Jesse Jackson and Ralph Nader in the U.S. Here in Canada, Maude Barlow, the eloquent and charismatic leader of the Council of Canadians, has become a thorn in the corporate side. With her books, her speeches, her council's growing membership, she has emerged as an irrepressible critic of corporate rule, and to the CEOs that makes her dangerous. That's why they have unleashed all their media attack dogs in an effort to bring her into disrepute. Simply to moan, "Oh, not Maude Barlow again!" is sometimes thought to be enough to dismiss her. Of course it isn't. She continues to command enormous public respect and support.

I had a taste of this kind of treatment myself back in the 1970s when I was writing a weekly labour column for *The Toronto Star*, the paper with the largest circulation in Canada. Since I also held a full-time PR job with a union at the time, and since I frequently used the column to snipe at business leaders, I naturally incurred their wrath.

They tried several times to persuade *The Star*'s then managing editor, Martin Goodman, to terminate my column; but Marty was that rarity in the upper echelons of journalism— an editor who refused to slavishly toe the corporate line. You might even say that Marty himself was a heretic, and after he snubbed my corporate critics for the umpteenth time, they finally gave up and I went on to write the column for 14 years, subjected only to occasional attacks on my credibility by the pro-business columnists.

But eventually the business barons got their revenge when Marty tragically died of cancer in 1982. He was barely in his grave when his successor as managing editor—someone obviously more acceptable than Marty to the business community—phoned to tell me curtly that my column was "no longer needed."

Now that I'm confined to writing for *The CCPA Monitor*, my views don't reach nearly enough people to make the CEOs uneasy. So I can safely be ignored. But Maude Barlow has a much higher profile. So does CAW economist and CCPA research associate Jim Stanford. So do authors Linda McQuaig and Murray Dobbin. So do a few others on the left like Tony Clarke, Neil Brooks, and Buzz Hargrove. Their prominence as dissenters makes them targets for more concentrated efforts to discredit them.

Until recently, such efforts would invariably succeed. Today, with the Internet serving as a powerful and (so far) non-corporate-controlled communication medium, and with the growing and increasingly effective coalitions of NGOs on the left, the élite's media substitute for the Inquisition may be losing its force.

Let's hope so. In the meantime, it's worth keeping in mind that, while Giordano Bruno still inspires and encourages us 400 years after his death, the names of his persecutors—even that of Pope Clement VIII, who ordered his execution—have long since been forgotten.❖

It all boils down to unfair distribution

When Mahatma Gandhi, more than half a century ago, remarked that "the world holds enough to satisfy everyone's need, but not everyone's greed," he was pithily identifying the main cause of most of the world's social and economic problems. And he was also pointing to their obvious solution.

Poverty, hunger, homelessness, illiteracy, preventable disease, polluted air and water, and most of the other ills that beset humanity have one root cause: the inequitable distribution of the planet's wealth and resources.

People who have enough money—no matter where they may live—are not poor, do not go hungry, do not lack shelter or a good education, and have access to quality health care.

Famines don't break out in posh residential districts. Business executives don't visit food banks or sleep under bridges. The rich can afford to stay healthy and live longer than the poor.

These simple truths are obvious. They underscore the equally obvious fact that the answer to most human misery and injustice is a fair allocation of the world's wealth.

Unfortunately, the economic system that now predominates in most parts of the world—laissez-faire capitalism— promotes, defends, and even extols an increasingly unequal distribution of wealth. Its three ideological principles are greed, individualism, and competition, all of which militate against economic and social justice.

So we have a system in which the three top executives of Microsoft control more wealth than all the people in the world's poorest 50 countries. We have 400 billionaires with more wealth than the poorest two-and-half billion people. And the proponents of this grossly inequitable system see nothing wrong with it. They would presumably not object if eventually 500 billionaires accumulated more wealth than 90% of the rest of humankind. That's what a free market is all about, they would tell us. In a system based on survival of the financially fittest, the financially unfit don't survive—and don't deserve to.

This application of the law of the jungle to human society is not new. It reigned supreme in the 1800s when the "robber barons" of business were free to exploit the world's resources and workers for their own enrichment and that of their shareholders. Poverty, hunger, and homelessness were rampant then, too, among the general population.

The first three-quarters of the 20th century, however, saw the emergence of governments and unions committed to the alleviation of poverty and hunger, and thus to a less inequitable distribution of income. Gradually, through most of the century, the lives of workers and their families—at least in the industrialized nations—were improved by the implementation of a wide range of social programs. And these programs were funded largely by taking larger and larger amounts from the coffers of the most affluent individuals and companies.

The lesson this redistributive approach taught us was that it was not necessary to get rid of capitalism or replace it with democratic socialism (as preferable as that change might be). It was possible to offset its inherently unfair distribution of income through socially progressive legislation, a fair tax system, and strong, government-supported unions.

It seemed for a while, especially in the first three decades after World War II, that corporate leaders and investors were resigned to these constraints on their greed. But in fact they always resented them, and were determined to break free of them whenever they could. That opportunity came in the mid-'70s with the simultaneous promotion of globalized "free" trade and the development of the new computer and communication technologies. Corporations were able to escape from national limits and boundaries—and from any compulsion to keep sharing their profits with society's less fortunate.

With their enormous increase in wealth came more power and influence, including the power to buy and control most politicians. From being agents of wealth distribution, governments were transformed into the legislative arms of big business, devoted to helping the rich become richer at the expense of everyone else.

The labour movement was not subverted, but, denied government backing and facing employers now willing and able to relocate to low-wage regions, most unions were weakened. Some still manage to extract more in wages than a company is willing to concede, but the redistributive role of organized labour has been reduced, and certainly cannot compensate for the massive withdrawal of governments from this important responsibility.

The free marketers try to argue that there just isn't enough money any more to finance social security. In fact, looking at the Canadian situation, this country's economy today generates one-and-a-half times more wealth—in per capita terms and in constant dollars—than it did in the early 1970s, when there was no question about our ability to afford the welfare state. All that's different now is that most of the extra money is being concentrated in fewer and fewer bank accounts.

The upshot is that the function of redistributing wealth is now mainly taking the form of charity. Thousands of charitable organizations now beg the corporations and the high- and middle-income earners to share some of their income with the needy. Appeals for charitable donations clog the mails, the airwaves, and the telephone lines. Motorists driving on city streets encounter schoolchildren at busy intersections begging for loonies to help save school programs threatened by government cutbacks.

All of the causes championed by charities are worthwhile. All of the hungry and destitute they help are deserving. But their growing dependence on handouts has two major flaws: it perpetuates (perhaps even institutionalizes) a system built on avarice and inequity; and it ensures that the problems of poverty and hunger will persist and even get worse because the proceeds of charity alone will never be enough to eliminate them.

In the euphoric aftermath of the "battle of Seattle" at the end of the 20th century, the victors in civil society may have felt they had the hardline free marketers on the run. But their success in preventing the rich and powerful from agreeing on how they could become even more rich and powerful—as laudable as it undeniably was—still leaves an already brutal and barbaric system intact.

It's important, as we fight these battles, always to keep the nature of both the problem and the solution in mind. The problem is an unfair distribution of wealth, and the solution—however it may be achieved—is a fair distribution of wealth. Any proposals or discussions that ignore that simple truth waste our time, squander our resources, and undermine our efforts to create a better world.❖

EPILOGUE
Costs, risks and sacrifices

Many Canadians still refuse to believe that they now live in a country where genuine democracy has given away to corporate tyranny. These are the people who still haven't joined the CCPA or the Council of Canadians, the people who haven't read the latest books by Linda McQuaig (*The Cult of Impotence*) and Murray Dobbin (*The Myth of the Good Corporate Citizen*), both of them guaranteed cures for credulity. Their well-documented story of the loss of Canadian democracy is guaranteed to open the eyes of the most gullible voters. No one, having read either, would doubt that it is the big corporations which now tell governments what to do, not the other way around.

It's easy for politicians to do what the business moguls want, even if it's harmful to the great majority of voters, because the voters have no real power in a corporatist state. All they can do is exchange one bunch of corporate flunkeys for another. In such a system, the adoption by governments of policies that displease their corporate masters is tantamount to political suicide.

Peter Newman, in his otherwise laudatory review of McQuaig's book for the *Globe and Mail*, pointed out that "breaking the rules [of globalization]" would bring down upon Canada the financial and economic hammer-blows of the world's new rulers, the TNCs. It would mean "going native"—"fighting to retain value—almost any value—for our pesos."

Newman himself thinks Canada has truly become impotent, and that "our impotence remains uncured and probably untreatable."

He's wrong, of course. But he's correct in his assessment of how formidable a task regaining our sovereignty really is. It indeed means exposing ourselves to the terribly punitive measures that the wielders of global wealth and power can inflict on us. The combined might of the banks, the money traders, the credit-rating agencies, the TNCs, the IMF, the World Bank, the WTO—and, let's not forget, the governments of the United States and other major countries committed to corporate rule—would strike us with brutal and merciless impact.

These retaliations wouldn't come all at once, of course. They would be applied incrementally, to test the strength of our resolve. The TNCs might assume we'd give up the fight for democracy at the first stages of their financial squeeze, or at least when the first wave of business shutdowns and lay-offs started. Only if we stood firm would the most damaging blows fall on us. The impacts would destabilize our economy, massively devalue our dollar, precipitate capital flights and capital strikes, and—initially, at least—triple our unemployment rate.

Could Canada survive such an assault? Yes, we could—if we had a majority of our citizens willing to defend our country, at any cost, any sacrifice. And if we had governments—provincial as well as federal—that would lead us in such an all-out economic war. Canada, after all, despite its current heavy dependence on trade and exports, is potentially a self-sufficient nation. We could, if we had to, produce all the necessities of life for all our people within our own borders.

We could even survive an embargo such as the one the U.S. has imposed on Cuba for the past 38 years. Canada is richer in resources than Cuba, and with the right policies could weather all the sanctions the U.S. could throw at us.

Admittedly, such a return to economic self-reliance would take many years and would come at a heavy price, initially, in terms of our living standards. It would also be contingent on the United States not invading Canada and forcibly suppressing our "resistance," as it has done in the past in Nicaragua, Grenada, Panama, Guatemala, and many other countries in the hemisphere that dared to antagonize Washington. (Even if the Marines were not sent in, we could almost certainly expect a concerted effort by the CIA to subvert and oust a "Marxist" Canadian government that so openly spurned U.S. hegemony.)

Before such a revolt against corporate global rule could even be contemplated, however, two enormously difficult preconditions would have to be put in place. The first, of course, is that most Canadians—preferably 75% or more—would have to be persuaded to support and participate in such a rebellion, in full knowledge of the risks and sacrifices that would be incurred. And secondly, a political party would have to emerge that would respond to this democratic resolve and have the courage to give the required legislative leadership.

McQuaig and Dobbin, together with Maude Barlow of the Council of Canadians and Tony Clarke of the Polaris Institute, and of course CCPA Executive Director Bruce Campbell and other researchers and activists affiliated with the Centre, are doing their best to fulfill the first requirement: public awareness. They assume, as I have, that when Canadians understand why and how their sovereignty has been usurped, they will be mad enough to fight for its recovery—and that this popular uprising will find (or create) an appropriate political outlet.

Are these safe or even plausible assumptions? Frankly, I don't know, and neither, I suspect, does anyone else. It could be that, even when fully informed, most Canadians would be more inclined to live under corporate rule than dare to challenge it. But one thing is clear: the struggle against the market-driven New World Order, if it is to develop and gain momentum, must begin with its exposure—and I can only hope that the foregoing essays will help some Canadians take that all-important first step.